Grammatical Concepts 101

for Biblical Hebrew

Learning Biblical Hebrew Grammatical Concepts through English Grammar

GARY A. LONG

HENDRICKSON PUBLISHERS

D

Grammatical Concepts 101 for Biblical Hebrew:
Learning Biblical Hebrew Grammatical Concepts through English Grammar
© 2002 by Hendrickson Publishers, Inc.
P. O. Box 3473
Peabody, Massachusetts 01961-3473

ISBN 978-1-56563-713-9

Printed in the United States of America

Fourth Printing — March 2009

Library of Congress Cataloging-in-Publication Data

Long, Gary A. (Gary Alan), 1959–
    Grammatical concepts 101 for Biblical Hebrew : learning Biblical Hebrew grammatical concepts through English grammar / Gary A. Long.
      p. cm.
    Includes bibliographical references and index.
    ISBN-13: 978-1-56563-713-9
    ISBN-10: 1-56563-713-5
    1. Hebrew language—Grammar.   2. English language—Grammar.   3. Bible. O.T.—Language, style.   I. Title.
    PJ4567.3 .L66 2002
    492.4′82421—dc21
                              2002005199

To the memory of

ROBERT L. ALDEN

TABLE OF CONTENTS

PART I: FOUNDATIONS

PART II: BUILDING BLOCKS

PART III: THE CLAUSE AND BEYOND

ACKNOWLEDGMENTS

My wonderful students who have walked the same path as I in wanting to learn Biblical Hebrew have been the inspiration behind this book. Hopefully, they will find it the help I want it to be for them.

I am indebted to the English Grammar Series (The Olivia and Hill Press) for the idea of illustrating English alongside a language to be learned. Brent Hagany, my faithful student assistant at Bethel College, deserves thanks for his careful reading of earlier drafts. I am grateful for the feedback I received from the prepublication use of this work at Harvard University. John Ellison, of that institution, offered advice that helped to recast some of the content's organization. John Cook generously shared unpublished work that has informed my treatment of aspect and tense related to Biblical Hebrew. John Kutsko, of Hendrickson, has guided this project through to publication with efficiency and grace. For that I am most appreciative. Each has brought improvement. Errors and insufficiencies that still remain, of course, are entirely my own doing.

Lifelong thanks go to my *Doktorvater,* Dennis Pardee, of the University of Chicago. It is he who patiently guided me through the foundations of my discipline in Northwest Semitic languages and Ancient Near Eastern studies—a discipline I have now been fortunate to have taught for a decade.

Robert Alden first introduced me to the world of the Hebrew Bible. A professor at Denver Seminary, he modeled a passion for embracing life—from teaching, to climbing all of the Rocky Mountains' "14ers" (twice, if not thrice). Death, a few years back, took him much too early. He saw me, seemingly, as a student needing help in speaking English more correctly. English is my mother tongue, but around Prof. Alden, I soon discovered that I, seemingly, had slept through lessons on grammar during high school and college. I remember well his stopping me often in mid-sentence to correct me. I saw it as a gesture born of his care. I think dedicating to his dear memory a book that teaches grammar is fitting.

Twin Cities   G. A. LONG
April 2002

INTRODUCTION

Designed to complement standard teaching grammars, this book assists the entry-level Biblical Hebrew student in learning basic grammatical concepts no single *teaching* grammar treats adequately and no *reference* grammar explains plainly enough for many beginning students. We revisit English grammar to accomplish this. After several years of teaching a variety of ancient Semitic languages, I recognize that most of my students have been learning two languages at the same time: the ancient language, of course, *and* the grammar and grammatical concepts of English, often forgotten.

I have written the book for a learner who has had little or no formal study of grammar. The language, therefore, strives for simplicity wherever possible. Some will find the language, at times, (overly)simplistic. I define nouns, for example, as words that name, rather than according to formal and functional criteria like case and number inflection, syntactic functions, distribution (they follow prepositions but not modals), etc. Others, still, may find the language, at times, a bit of a challenge. You, the reader, will see abundant English and Hebrew examples illustrating each concept, most of them **visually** analyzed. A gloss (a literal, word-by-word English equivalent of the Hebrew) and translation assist the comprehension of the Hebrew examples.

The concepts in this book are arranged from the more basic to the more involved. Part I, *Foundations,* contains concepts that lie at the very foundation of language. Part II, *Building Blocks,* treats concepts in an order similar to many teaching grammars. Here the learner can augment a teaching grammar's presentation. Part III, *The Clause and Beyond,* introduces the learner to the higher levels of language.

This resource is not comprehensive in subject matter, and it does not show the full variety of ways Biblical Hebrew may convey a particular concept. Many of the concepts I address are more completely analyzed in Biblical Hebrew reference grammars. Consult them as you become more familiar with grammar and as your ability to read Hebrew increases over time.[1] They are *indispensable*.

Tips for Learning Biblical Hebrew

1. **Memory.** Your memory plays an important role in learning a language. You will spend many hours memorizing vocabulary, paradigms, grammatical rules, and the like. Here are some thoughts that may help you with those tasks.

   - Divide the lesson into learnable sections.

   - Read each section aloud several times.

   - Rewrite the section word for word or in your own words.

   - Compare what you have written with the textbook.

2. **Vocabulary.** Each of us brings different abilities to the learning process. In learning a language you will likely learn a lot about yourself—what works for you, what does not. Some strategies will work, some will not. Try a lot of things and stick with anything that helps you learn. Here is what other learners have tried.

   - Write each word on a blank vocabulary card: Hebrew on one side, English on the other.

   - Use cards of different color to assist you with helpful classifications: gender of nominals (one color for masculine, another for feminine nouns), or parts of speech (one color for verbs, another for adjectives).

   - Flip through the cards reading the Hebrew aloud, then think of the English gloss (= literal translation). Flip through the cards reading the

---

[1] For example, Bruce K. Waltke and M. O'Connor, *An Introduction to Biblical Hebrew Syntax* (Winona Lake, Ind.: Eisenbrauns, 1990); Paul Joüon, *A Grammar of Biblical Hebrew* (trans. and revised by T. Muraoka; 2 vols.; *Subsidia biblica* 14/1–2; Rome: Pontificio Istituto Biblico, 1993); Christo H. J. van der Merwe, Jackie A. Naudé, and Jan H. Kroeze, *A Biblical Hebrew Reference Grammar* (Biblical Languages: Hebrew 3; Sheffield: Sheffield Academic Press, 1999).

English saying the Hebrew aloud. Shuffle the cards so that you do not become too reliant on order and placement.

- Most Biblical Hebrew words have a foundation, usually of three *root* consonants. This means that most all words that share the same root are related in meaning—they share a *linkedness* or *connectedness*. The root is usually composed of three consonants. For example, you will learn the nouns מֶלֶךְ *king* and מַלְכָּה *queen*. You will learn verbal forms like מָלַךְ *he ruled* and מָלַכְתִּי *I ruled*. The root מלכ√/MLK underlies the words. Get the connection? Try grouping vocabulary cards by their common root.

3. **Assignments.** Keep up with the assignments. Do not let yourself fall behind. Morale, to say nothing of grades, can nose dive when you do not keep pace.

Part I
Foundations

LINGUISTIC HIERARCHIES

A helpful way to view language is to see it as a fusion of the abstract (**EMIC**) with the tangible (**ETIC**). Think of a word in your head. Now think of an entire sentence. Think of a few more things you could say. No one knows what you have just thought. This *emic* realm of language is abstract, not tangible, existing only in your mind. The emic is the conceptual realm of language.

Now say aloud what you had in your mind, or take a pen and write it down. This *etic* realm of language is physically represented when one speaks or writes (or gestures, if one communicates through sign language). Language is *physically* produced through sounds or *phones* (see below) or writing symbols, *graphs.* These sounds and written symbols are the building blocks of words, phrases, and clauses that can be conveyed to another person.

We can break down language into building blocks or hierarchies. Each of the following units, listed from smallest to largest (bottom to top in Figure i), has an emic and etic realm. I find the term **EXPRESSION** convenient to refer to a written or oral articulation of language at the level of word or higher when I do not have a specific level in mind.

EMIC	ETIC
emic discourse or text	etic discourse or text
emic paragraph	etic paragraph
emic sentence	etic sentence or utterance
emic clause	etic clause
emic phrase	etic phrase
emic word lexical item	etic word or lexical item
lexeme	lex
morpheme	morph
phoneme	phone

Figure i: Linguistic Hierarchies

PHONE(ME) is a sound or speech unit that is psychologically a single unit and that makes a difference. Make a /z/ sound, as in **z**ebra. Now make a /v/ sound, as in **v**ictory. The sounds or speech units /z/ and /v/ are psychologically each a single unit and each makes a difference. The first word, after all, makes no sense if we say **v**ebra; and **z**ictory is equally nonsensical. בֶּלֶךְ does not clearly communicate that you mean to say מֶלֶךְ. Linguists use slashed lines to represent phonemes. These abstract units often have variations when articulated as phones. Sounds next to each other, whether another consonant or a vowel, can affect each other. These variations are known as **ALLOPHONES**. For example, hold your hand close to your mouth and say the words *pin* and *spin*. Notice that the /p/ of *pin* includes a more explosive burst of air than the /p/ of *spin*.

MORPH(EME) is the *smallest* or *minimal* block of language that is *meaningful* and recurrent for word-building in a language. The notion of *meaningful* is important. A phone(me) is the smallest block but it does not convey meaning. What, after all, does /b/ mean? It does not *mean* anything. All sorts of concepts are conveyed in morphemes: plurality, singularity, tense, gender, etc. Morphemes may have variations known as **ALLOMORPHS**. For example, the morpheme 'plural of a noun' has the allomorphs -*s* (cat*s*), -*z* (lid*s*), and -*əz* (for*ces*). In Hebrew, the morpheme 'feminine' is conveyed through the allomorphs הָ- and ת- for singular nominals (see **NOMINAL**, p. 36).

LEX(EME) is the typically foundational element of a word or lexical item. The idea of a lex(eme) is not the easiest to comprehend in English, but it is typically represented as the dictionary form of any word. For example, a person learning English may encounter the word *kicked* in a text; the dictionary will have the word entered simply as *kick*. *Kick*, as represented on the page is

4

the *lex*, while the concept behind the word is the *lexeme*. The notion of lexemes is simpler in Biblical Hebrew. The consonantal root underlying a word may be considered the lexeme; for example, the root √MLK is the lexeme underlying מֶ֫לֶךְ *king* or מַלְכָּה *queen*.

WORD
is a language building block composed of a lexeme and all morphemes. For example, the etic lexical item or word *kicked* is composed, in part, of the lexeme 'kick' plus the morpheme 'past tense', reflected in the morph *-ed*. Parsing in Biblical Hebrew is actually accounting for the lexemic and morphemic composition of a lexical item. The etic verb form כָּתְבָה *she wrote* is composed of the lexeme √KTB plus the morphemes 'Qal', 'Suffix (Perfect) Conjugation', 'third person', 'feminine', and 'singular'.

PHRASE
is a language unit referring to a string of words (a *syntagm*)—two or more—that does not involve predication (see **PREDICATE/PREDICATION**, p. 127); it does not have a subject and a predicate together.

in the house   בַּבַּ֫יִת

a small book   סֵ֫פֶר קָטָן

                                  small   book

CLAUSE
is a language unit referring to a string of words (a *syntagm*) that involves predication. See **CLAUSE**, p. 123.

SENTENCE
is a language unit referring to a string of words that involves predication and that in Biblical Hebrew is typically composed of one independent clause and all modifying subordinate clauses. By this definition, a sentence composed of only one independent unmodified clause is both a clause and a sentence.

A sentence, however, is a difficult and somewhat arbitrary concept to define, particularly for a *linking/chaining* language like Biblical Hebrew. Main clause after main clause may be linked by the conjunction *and/*ו. Biblical Hebrew can have several verbal clauses joined with *vav* but share a single subject or adverbial or adjectival element.

PARAGRAPH   is a language unit that in Biblical Hebrew is typically composed of two or more sentences usually with a similar topic. Two or more sentences may be equally prominent or prominent sentences may occur along with modifying sentences (such as reason or result).

DISCOURSE   is the highest of the linguistic hierarchies typically composed of a large "chunk" of text. See **DISCOURSE ANALYSIS**, p. 151.

SOUND PRODUCTION

Speech **SOUNDS** or **SEGMENTS** are the fundamental components of a spoken language. Created along the **VOCAL TRACT** (the area between the vocal folds and lips), they tend to be classified according to the amount of obstruction involved in producing them. Vowel sounds are generally produced with less obstruction than consonantal sounds. The following discussion has Biblical Hebrew primarily in mind.

CONSONANTS

PLACE OF ARTICULATION, MANNER OF ARTICULATION, and **VOICING** are concepts commonly associated with producing consonants. The classifications and sound descriptions I use below follow a *Modern Israeli Ashkenazi Hebrew* pronunciation—the commonest pronunciation one hears throughout Israel. Acquiring a modern Israeli pronunciation for Biblical Hebrew will provide you with a good foundation in case you pursue further studies in Hebrew. The Hebrew spoken by the writers of the Hebrew Bible sounded similar but not the same as the modern pronunciation.

PLACE OF ARTICULATION

The place of articulation is the point in the vocal tract where the greatest constriction or obstruction occurs (see Figure ii below). The Biblical Hebrew consonants include the following articulatory places.

Labials	consonants formed by the lips
Bilabials	consonants formed by the two lips together
Labiodentals	consonants formed with the lower lip tucked just behind the upper front teeth
Dentals	consonants formed with the tip of the tongue touching the back of the upper front teeth (no Hebrew consonant is precisely a dental, though many grammar books

7

	classify some as such; Hebrew consonants classified as dentals are more appropriately alveolars)
Alveolars	consonants formed with the tip of the tongue raised to the bony ridge immediately behind the teeth, the alveolar ridge
Palatals	consonants formed with the blade and center of the tongue raised to the hard palate
Velars	consonants formed with the center and dorsum of the tongue raised to the velum or soft palate
Uvulars	consonants formed with the dorsum of the tongue raised to the uvula
Pharyngeals	consonants formed in the upper pharyngeal cavity (Modern Israeli Ashkenazi pronunciation has no pharyngeal, but Modern Israeli *Sephardi* produces the ע as a pharyngeal)
Glottals	consonants formed in the glottal region, the opening between the vocal folds

MANNER OF ARTICULATION

The vocal tract can affect airflow. Manner of articulation refers to the manner or way that the sound is produced, usually in terms of the amount of constriction the airflow encounters. Biblical Hebrew has **OBSTRUENTS** and the **SONORANTS**.

Obstruent	a distinctive feature that characterizes speech sound when airflow is constricted
Plosive/Stop	obstruent consonant sound made by temporarily blocking the airflow completely
Fricative	obstruent consonant sound in which the airflow is channeled through a narrow opening in the speech path

Within the fricative category you should take note of the SIBILANTS. Higher frequency energy is required to produce sibilants, giving them a hissing sound. The sibilants are ז, ס, צ, שׁ, and שׂ.

Affricative obstruent consonant sound in which the airflow for a single consonant consists of a plosive/stop followed by a secondary fricative release

Trill obstruent consonant sound where vibration occurs; the Modern Israeli Ashkenazi Hebrew pronunciation of syllable-initial /r/ is a fricative to which vibration is added

Sonorant a distinctive feature that characterizes speech sound whose articulation is not so narrow that the airflow across the glottis is appreciably inhibited

Nasal sonorant consonant sound made with a lowered velum, thus engaging the natural resonance of the nasal passages—the oral cavity is closed so that air flows through the nasal cavity.

Liquid sonorant consonant sound in which the speech path is neither closed off nor constricted to a degree that produces friction

Under the label of liquids, Biblical Hebrew has a

Lateral consonant (/l/), where the tip of the tongue is raised to the alveolar ridge but the sides of the tongue are down permitting the air to flow laterally over the sides of the tongue.

Glide sonorant consonant vowel-like sounds that precede or follow a true vowel

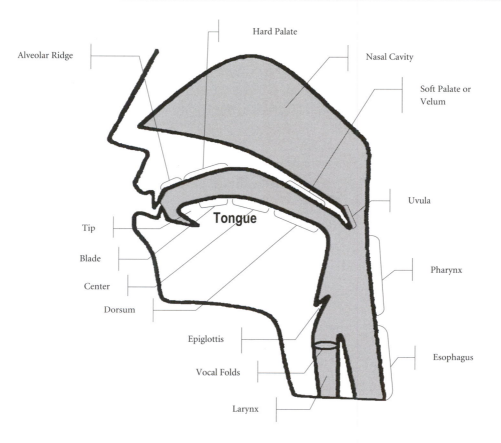

Figure ii: Places of Articulation

VOICING

Voicing refers to the vibration of the vocal folds during the production of a sound. If the vocal folds are tense and the airflow from the lungs forces them to vibrate, the consonantal sounds are **VOICED**. If the air flows freely through the relaxed vocal folds into the supraglottal speech organs, the consonantal sounds are **VOICELESS**.

We are ready to describe the consonants.

	PLACE	VOICING	MANNER
א	glottal	voiceless	plosive
בּ	bilabial	voiced	plosive
ב	labiodental	voiced	fricative
גּ ג	velar	voiced	plosive
דּ ד	alveolar	voiced	plosive
ה	glottal	voiceless	fricative
ו	labiodental	voiced	fricative
ז	alveolar	voiced	fricative
ח	velar	voiceless	fricative
ט	alveolar	voiceless	plosive
י	alveopalatal	voiced	glide
כּ	velar	voiceless	plosive
ך כ	velar	voiceless	fricative
ל	alveolar	voiced	lateral
ם מ	bilabial	voiceless	nasal
ן נ	alveolar	voiced	nasal
ס	alveolar	voiceless	fricative
ע	glottal	voiceless	plosive
פּ	bilabial	voiceless	plosive
ף פ	labiodental	voiceless	fricative
ץ צ	alveolar	voiceless	affricate
ק	velar	voiceless	plosive

ר	uvular	voiced	fricative trill
	Resh is commonly pronounced in this fashion when it is the onset of a syllable (=syllable-initial). When it occurs as the coda of a syllable (=syllable-final), the trill commonly does not occur but the throat is constricted at the uvula		
שׂ	alveolar	voiceless	fricative
שׁ	alveopalatal	voiceless	fricative
תּ ת	alveolar	voiceless	plosive

Figure iii: Phonetic Classification of Consonants

VOWELS

Vowel sounds have little obstruction in Biblical Hebrew. For vowels we distinguish **QUALITY** (or **TIMBRE**), the difference in vowel sound production along the speech path, and **QUANTITY** (or **DURATION** or **LENGTH**), the actual time involved in producing the vowel sound. Further, **TONGUE POSITION** and **LIP POSITION** are important factors.

A **SIMPLE** (or **PURE**) vowel refers to one with a single sound. A **DIPHTHONG** is a sequence of two sounds consisting of a simple vowel plus a glide consonant (י).

TONGUE POSITION

Here one may note (1) the height of the tongue and (2) the part of the tongue involved. The tongue height may be **HIGH**, **MID**, or **LOW**; the part of the tongue used may be the **FRONT** (tip and blade), **CENTER**, and **BACK** (dorsum). For example, the vowel sound in the English word

*b*ee*t* is high and front;

*b*oo*t* is high and back;

*h*o*t* is low and back;

*b*oa*t* is mid and back;

12

*bou*ght is between mid and low and back;

*cu*p is mid and central.

LIP POSITION

Vowel sounds differ depending on whether the lips are rounded. For example, in the previous paragraph, the vowel in *boot* was characterized as high and back, but it also entails lip rounding, while *hot* (low and back) has an unrounded vowel.

PUTTING THE PIECES TOGETHER

The charts below combine the features we use to describe the vowels of Biblical Hebrew. The Hebrew Bible we read is called the Masoretic Text (MT) or Tiberian Hebrew. The Masoretes were scholars who developed a series of symbols to represent vowel sounds and added them to the much older text written only with consonants (some of those consonants, though, doubled as vowel sounds: ה, ו, י). This process occurred around 700 C.E.

The MT has seven vowel *qualities* (or *timbres*). In Tiberian Hebrew, vowel *quantity* (or *length*) likely plays no role, though many Hebrew grammars talk of long and short vowels. The seven vowel qualities, though, do not contain vowels that are pronounced for a longer duration than others. Those seven vowel timbres of Tiberian Hebrew can be classified as follows:

Tongue Height	**Part of Tongue**		
	Front	Center	Back
	unrounded		rounded
High	/i/(= ִ , ִי)		/u/(= ֻ , וּ)
	/e/(= ֵ , ֵי , ֵה)		
Mid	/ɛ/(= ֶ , ֶי , ֶה)		/o/(= ֹ , וֹ)
		/æ/(= ַ)	
Low		/a/(= ָ , ָה)	

Figure iv: Classification of Tiberian Vowel Phonemes

The Tiberian Hebrew phoneme (see **PHONE[ME]** under **LINGUISTIC HIERARCHIES**, p. 3):

/i/(= ִ , ִי) was pronounced generally as [i] as in *mach***i***ne.*

/e/(= ֵ , ֵי , ֵה) was pronounced generally as [e] in *th***ey***.*

/ɛ/(= ֶ , ֶי , ֶה) was pronounced generally as [ɛ] in *b***e***t.*

/æ/(= ַ) was pronounced generally as [æ] in *th***a***t.*

/a/(= ָ , ָה) was pronounced generally as [a] in *f***a***ther.*

/o/(= ֹ , וֹ) was pronounced generally as [o] in *n***o***te.*

/u/(= ֻ , וּ) was pronounced generally as [u] in *m***oo***d.*

Modern Hebrew pronunciation, which many Biblical Hebrew instructors use, has only five simple vowel timbres reflecting the seven in Tiberian Hebrew. Vowel quantity or length, like Tiberian Hebrew, plays no role. The next chart traces the correspondences.

Tiberian Phonemes & Transliterations	Modern Hebrew Phonemes		
/i/ = i, $\hat{i}$ or i^y	/i/ (= i, $\hat{i}$ or i^y) pronounced as [i] in *machine*		
/e/ = $\bar{e}$, $\hat{e}$ or $\bar{e}^y$, ה $\bar{e}^h$	/ɛ/	(= $\bar{e}$, $\hat{e}$ or $\bar{e}^y$, ה $\bar{e}^h$)	pronounced as [ɛ] in *bet* [2]
/ɛ/ = e, $\hat{e}$ or e^y, ה e^h		(= e, $\hat{e}$ or e^y, ה e^h)	
/æ/ = a	/a/	(= a)	pronounced as [a] in *father*
/a/ = $\bar{a}$, ה $\bar{a}^h$, א $\bar{a}^{\,\prime}$		(= $\bar{a}$, ה $\bar{a}^h$, א $\bar{a}^{\,\prime}$)	
/o/ = $\bar{o}$, ו $\hat{o}$ or $\bar{o}^w$	/o/	(= o in a closed, unaccented syllable)	pronounced as [o] in *note*
		(= $\bar{o}$, ו $\hat{o}$ or $\bar{o}^w$)	
/u/ = u, ו $\hat{u}$ or u^w	/u/ (= u, ו $\hat{u}$ or u^w) pronounced as [u] in *mood*		

Figure v: Correspondence of the Tiberian Phonemes and Transliterations to the Five Modern Hebrew Phonemes

---

[2] You will also hear individual speakers pronounce this timbre as [e] in *they*.

SYLLABLE

A **SYLLABLE** is a sound or phonological unit composed of (1) an **ONSET**, (2) a **NUCLEUS**, and it may have (3) a **CODA**.

ENGLISH

In the English *bed*, /b/ is the onset, /ɛ/ is the nucleus, and /d/ is the coda.

BIBLICAL HEBREW

In Biblical Hebrew, syllables *must* begin with a consonant, that is, they must have a consonant onset. **No syllable in Biblical Hebrew ever begins with a vowel** (except the conjunction *vav* when vocalized as וּ). A syllable in Biblical Hebrew may be either **OPEN** or **CLOSED**.

> An *open* syllable ends in a vowel (Cv = Consonant, followed by *v*owel). It has an onset (C-) and a nucleus (-v-), but no coda.

    דָּבָר / דָּ   *dā* / *bar*   The first syllable is open, Cv.
      word

> A *closed* syllable ends in a consonant (CvC). It has an onset (C-), a nucleus (-v-) and a coda (-C).

    דָּבָר / דָּ   *dā* / *b̄ar*   The second syllable is closed, CvC.
      word

TRANSLATION[3]

What is happening when two people talk or write? They are, in part, encoding and decoding a code. This is likely not the answer you readily had in mind, but let us explore this.

Language involves at least two concepts:

➤ FORM, or to be more linguistically technical, CODE, and

➤ MEANING.

A code alone does not communicate. An unknown language can sound or look like a jumble of nothing—remember what a page of Biblical Hebrew first looked like to you! Every language has its own specific system for linking its code, that is, linking its form with meaning. A spoken and written language has a:

➤ PHONOLOGY, a system of sounds. If the language is written, these sounds are connected with a writing system.

➤ LEXICON, that is, a vocabulary.

➤ GRAMMAR, a set of patterns for making meaningful expressions.

MEANING is universal. Though different cultures may organize and conceive things differently, we share many things. For example, many cultures express casual greetings. In the morning, those who speak English may convey the greetings as "Good morning." "Good morning" is the FORM English speakers use to convey a *meaning*ful greetings. Form is the unique pattern of a specific language.

Each language has its own distinctive form, and the same meaning may be expressed in another language in quite a different form. "Good morning" is an adjective preceding a common noun. A Modern Hebrew speaker might say *boqer tov* (literally: "morning good"), a grammatically masculine and singular common

---

[3] A version of this chapter appears in my *Old Testament Exegesis: Graduate Study Guide* (Springfield, Mo.: Global University, forthcoming).

noun followed by a grammatically masculine singular adjective. In Nigeria, in Hausa, one might say *Ina kwana?* "How's sleep?" Again, form is the unique pattern of a specific language.

I have been talking about the word "mean(ing)," let me use it to illustrate something. Consider the following expressions.

1. That was no mean (**insignificant**) accomplishment.

2. They are so mean (**cruel**) to me.

3. This will mean (**result in**) the end of our regime.

4. This means so much (**is so important**) to me.

5. I mean (**intend**) to help if I can.

6. Keep Off the Grass! This means (**refers to**) you.

7. Those clouds mean (**are a sign of**) rain.

8. She doesn't mean (**believe**) what she said.

These expressions illustrate that one form or pattern, in this case the letters M-E-A-N, can express different meanings.

Now, consider the following expressions.

1. Is this seat taken?

2. May I sit here?

3. Is this seat empty?

These are three different forms to express one meaning, namely, to express the intent of a person wanting to sit. Different forms may thus express one similar, if not identical, meaning.

In working with languages, you will quickly discover that expressions that retain similar form may actually express very different meanings. Consider the English expression "His heart is cold," which can mean "He is unfeeling." When transferred word for word, literally, into Mambila (a language in Nigeria), the meaning becomes in that language "He is peaceful." When the same is done into Cinyanja (a language in Zambia), the meaning is "He is afraid."[4] Hopefully, you see a problem here. Very different meanings might arise for an expression transferred word for word into another language.

The starting point of translation is the **SOURCE LANGUAGE** (SL). For the Hebrew Bible, the source languages are Biblical Hebrew and Aramaic. A translation should attempt to re-express the SL *meaning* into a **TARGET LANGUAGE** (TL).

By now you have seen that *form* in each language is unique. Thus, translation must entail a change in form. This change in form does not matter provided that the *meaning* of the message is unchanged.

Translation is not simply a process of only taking SL words or phrases and transferring them into similar TL words and phrases. That is,

SL:	word/phrase	word/phrase	word/phrase
	↕	↕	↕
TL:	word/phrase	word/phrase	word/phrase

This is known as a **GLOSS** among translators. It is not the same as a translation.

The translation task, rather, is one of understanding the forms of the SL and distilling the meaning from the SL vocabulary and grammar and re-expressing that meaning into TL forms that convey the equivalent SL meaning. Thus

---

[4] Examples come from Katharine Barnwell, *Introduction to Semantics and Translation* (2d ed.; Horsley Green, England: Summer Institute of Linguistics, 1980), 12.

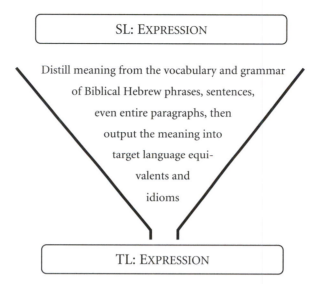

You must discover the meaning of the source language, in this case, Biblical Hebrew, and convey that meaning through the appropriate form of the target language, English.

TRANSLATIONS

Since language involves both form and meaning, and if we set these two on a continuum, we are able to characterize translations according to how form-oriented or meaning-oriented they are.

FORM-ORIENTED translations try to follow the form of the SL and are known as *literal*.

MEANING-ORIENTED ones are known as *idiomatic* or *dynamic equivalent*. Here is a continuum for characterizing some English translations.

FORM   MEANING

COMPLETELY LITERAL	MODIFIED LITERAL		IDIOMATIC		
Interlinear	KJV NASB	NRSV	NIV NAB	GNB NJB	CEV

COMPLETELY LITERAL. An interlinear is completely literal, completely form-oriented. Its value lies in showing the exegete the precise word order and other forms of the SL. Here is a completely literal presentation of 2 Samuel 7:1:

> "And-it-was when-sat the-king in-house-his and-Yahweh caused-rest-to-him from-around from-all-enemies-his."

MODIFIED LITERAL. These translations modify the form of the SL just to the extent that sentence structure is acceptable in the TL. Individual words, however, tend to be translated literally. The result is that though sentence structure is correct, the translation may not sound natural and may not convey meaning clearly. Here is a modified literal translation of 2 Samuel 7:1:

> "And it came about when the king lived in his house, and the LORD had given him rest from all his enemies all around, . . ."

Notice that sentence structure is not wrong, but to a native English speaker, the expression "And it came about" and a king living in a "house" (not a palace) sound less than natural.

IDIOMATIC. These translations strive to use natural forms—grammatical constructions *and* words—of the TL to convey the meaning of the SL. A truly idiomatic translation will sound like it was written originally in the TL; it will not sound like a translation. This is the goal of most Bible translators today entrusted with the task of providing Scriptures to groups who still do not have a translation of the Bible. Here is an idiomatic translation of 2 Samuel 7:1:

> "When the king had settled into his palace and the LORD had given him rest from all the enemies surrounding him, . . ."

TRANSLATING HOMEWORK IN FIRST-YEAR BIBLICAL HEBREW COURSES

As you begin trying to express Biblical Hebrew into English, you will likely be very form-oriented. This, at first, is not a bad idea. It allows your instructor to see that you are understanding the Hebrew form and patterns. As the year continues, though, and as you gain confidence in the language, strive for a meaning-oriented translation.

Part II
Building Blocks

GENDER

GENDER in language refers to classifying words usually as **MASCULINE, FEMININE,** or **NEUTER**. It plays an important structural role in many languages, but not in English. Nouns and verbs, in fact, have no special markings (morphs) for gender. In Biblical Hebrew gender is important and plays a role in nouns, verbs, and pronouns.

ENGLISH

Though English nouns and verbs have no special markings for gender, *nouns* typically reflect their biological sex. Male entities are *masculine.* Female entities are *feminine.* Other things tend to be *neuter.* When we replace a noun with a pronoun, we assign it gender.

➢ We use masculine pronouns to replace nouns that refer to males.

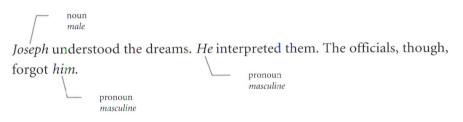

Joseph understood the dreams. *He* interpreted them. The officials, though, forgot *him.*

➢ We use feminine pronouns to replace nouns that refer to females.

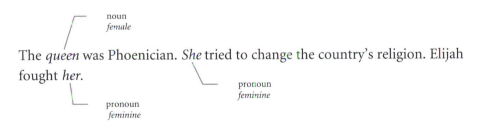

The *queen* was Phoenician. *She* tried to change the country's religion. Elijah fought *her.*

➢ We commonly, but not always, use the neuter pronoun *it* to replace all other nouns.

Workmen chiseled the *tunnel.* Water flowed through *it.*

25

But notice exceptions:

The great *ocean liner* left port. *She* was grand.

BIBLICAL HEBREW

All nouns in Biblical Hebrew are either *masculine* or *feminine*. Verbal forms also account for gender.

NOUNS

Most nouns that have no special marking (morph) are masculine, though quite a few are feminine. Nouns that refer to body parts that naturally occur in pairs tend to be feminine.

דָּבָר	word (masculine)	אֹזֶן	ear (feminine)
סוּס	horse (masculine)	זְרוֹעַ	arm (feminine)

Singular (see **NUMBER**, p. 27) feminine nouns are commonly marked with an ending: הָ - or ת-.

סוּסָה	mare	בְּרִית	covenant
מַלְכָּה	queen	דַּעַת	knowledge

VERBS

The verbal forms in Suffix (Perfect) and Prefix (Imperfect) Conjugations agree with the gender of the noun that functions as the subject in the clause. Exceptions do occur, but not often.

NUMBER

NUMBER, as a grammatical concept, refers to the quantity of participants involved with a word. When a word has only *one* participant, we call it SINGULAR. When a word has more than one participant, the word is PLURAL. Some languages, like Biblical Hebrew, have words that are DUAL, *two* participants.

➢ Nouns that allow us to enumerate the number of participants are known as COUNTABLE NOUNS.

➢ Nouns that are singular in form yet refer to a group are COLLECTIVE NOUNS.

➢ Verbs convey number, usually agreeing with the number of the grammatical subject of the clause.

ENGLISH

We form the plural of (countable) nouns in a variety of ways.

➢ add *-s* or *-es* to a singular noun

path	path*s*
kiss	kiss*es*

➢ more substantial changes

man	m*e*n
child	child*ren*
mouse	m*ice*

➢ no change

sheep	sheep

Collective nouns are singular in form yet refer to a group. American and British English speakers treat collective nouns differently. Americans generally use a verb that is singular while the British commonly use one that is plural.

➤ American English

　The *team is* winning.

➤ British English

　The *team are* winning.

BIBLICAL HEBREW

The forms (morphs) that convey number are sensitive to gender. Hebrew nouns convey singular, dual, and plural.

	Masculine	Feminine
Singular	no ending	◌ָה- or ◌ת-
Dual	◌ַיִם-	◌ַיִם-
Plural	◌ִים-	ות-

The dual, though, is restricted to nouns that

➤ occur in natural pairs (like hands);

　רֶגֶל foot　　　　　　　רַגְלַיִם two feet

➤ convey certain expressions of time;

　יוֹם day　　　　　　　יוֹמַיִם two days

➤ measure *two*.

　שְׁנַיִם two

The verbal forms of the Suffix (Perfect) and Prefix (Imperfect) Conjugations convey only singular and plural.

See your grammar textbook for more details.

28

ARTICLE

An **ARTICLE** stipulates whether a nominal is *unspecified* or *specified*.

ENGLISH

INDEFINITE ARTICLE

An indefinite article is placed before a nominal when it does *not* specify a particular person, animal, place, thing, event, or idea.

➤ English places an *a* before a word that begins with a consonantal sound.

Naomi saw *a* relative.

not a specified relative

➤ English places an *an* before a word that begins with a vowel sound.

Elijah looked at *an* altar.

not a specified altar

DEFINITE ARTICLE

A definite article is placed before a nominal when it specifies a particular person, animal, place, thing, event, or idea. English has one definite article, ***the***.

Elijah looked at *the* altar.

a specified altar

BIBLICAL HEBREW

INDEFINITE ARTICLE

Biblical Hebrew does not have an indefinite article. Any word that does not have a definite article, which Biblical Hebrew *does* have, ought to be conveyed in English with an indefinite article.

דָּבָר   וַיֹּאמֶר   He spoke *a word.*

word and-he-spoke

DEFINITE ARTICLE

The concept of definiteness in Biblical Hebrew is most commonly conveyed through an *attachment* placed on the front of a word. Stated somewhat more technically, the morpheme (see **MORPH[EME]** in the chapter **LINGUISTIC HIERARCHIES**, p. 3) of 'definiteness' is conveyed through a morph prefixed on a nominal. The *principal form* is הַ plus a doubling of the first consonant of the word to which the definite article is prefixed. Your grammar textbook likely lists the variations. Consult it.

הַשָּׁמָיִם	אֵת	אֱלֹהִים	בָּרָא	God created *the* heavens.
the-heavens	DO	God	he-created	Genesis 1:1

CONJUNCTION

A **CONJUNCTION** is a word that links words, phrases, and clauses. We speak of two types of conjunctions: **COORDINATING** and **SUBORDINATING**.

➤ coordinating conjunctions

Coordinate conjunctions join words, phrases, and clauses that are equal, connecting elements of equal status.

➤ subordinating conjunctions

Subordinate conjunctions join **DEPENDENT/SUBORDINATE** clauses to main clauses (see **CLAUSE**, p. 123).

CONJUNCTION OR PREPOSITION?

Some conjunctions also function as prepositions. When the word in question introduces a *clause*, the word is functioning as a *conjunction*. When the word does *not* introduce a clause, the word is functioning as a *preposition*. You will find examples below under the English and Biblical Hebrew sections.

ENGLISH

COORDINATING CONJUNCTIONS

The primary coordinating conjunctions in English are *and, but,* and *or.*

➤ words

heaven *and* earth

➤ phrases

in the city *but* outside the house

➤ clauses

Samuel came to Eli *but* Eli sent him back.

SUBORDINATING CONJUNCTIONS

Some primary subordinating conjunctions in English are *because, if, although, unless, while,* and *that.*

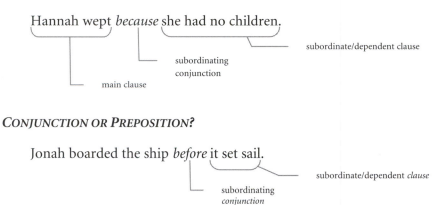

CONJUNCTION OR PREPOSITION?

Jonah boarded the ship *before* it set sail.

subordinate/dependent *clause*

subordinating *conjunction*

Jonah boarded the ship *before* noon.

object of the preposition

preposition

BIBLICAL HEBREW

COORDINATING CONJUNCTIONS

The primary coordinating conjunctions in Biblical Hebrew are וְ and אוֹ.

➤ words

וְהַיִּצְהָר   וְהַתִּירוֹשׁ   הַדָּגָן   the grain *and* the must *and* the oil

and-the-oil   *and*-the-must   the-grain   Hosea 2:10

➤ phrases

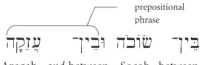

prepositional phrase

עֲזֵקָה   וּבֵין־   שׂוֹכֹה   בֵּין־   between Socoh *and* (between) Azeqah

Azeqah   *and*-between   Socoh   between   1 Samuel 17:1

➤ clauses

אֶבֶן וַיְקַלַּע   מִשָּׁם   וַיִּקַּח

and-he-slung stone from-there *and*-he-took

He took from there a stone
and slung it.

1 Samuel 17:49

SUBORDINATING CONJUNCTIONS

Some of the primary subordinating conjunctions in Biblical Hebrew are אִם,
אֲשֶׁר, כִּי, and לְמַעַן.

CONJUNCTION OR PREPOSITION?

As in English, be careful not to confuse when a form is functioning as a conjunction or a preposition.

dependent/subordinate *clause*

subordinating
conjunction

מָתְנוּ עַד־ פֹּה יֹשְׁבִים אֲנַחְנוּ מָה

we-die *until* here sitting we what

Why are we sitting here *until* we die?

2 Kings 7:3

object of the preposition

preposition

הָרָן עַד־ וַיָּבֹאוּ

Haran *until* and-they-came

They came *as far as* Haran.

Genesis 11:31

CATALOG OF THE SEMANTIC CONNECTIONS OF CONJUNCTIONS

Temporal or Chronological Conjunctions

אָז	then	כִּי	when
אַחַר	after, following	לִפְנֵי	before
אַחֲרֵי (אֲשֶׁר/כֵן)	after	עַד	until
(בְּ)טֶרֶם	before	עַד־אֲשֶׁר	before
וְ	then	עַתָּה	now
כַּאֲשֶׁר	when		

Logical Conjunctions

Continuative

אָז	then	גַּם	moreover, also
אַף	also	וְ	and, then, further

Contrast

אֲבָל	rather	וְ	but
אוֹ	or	וְ ... וְ	either . . . or
אַךְ	nevertheless, but	כִּי	rather
אֶפֶס	nevertheless, but	רַק	only

Purpose

לְמַעַן (אֲשֶׁר)   in order that, so that

Result

אֲשֶׁר	so that	לְמַעַן	so that
כִּי	so that	עַל־כֵּן	as a result
לָכֵן	as a result		

Inference

כֵּן	thus
לָכֵן	therefore
עַל־כֵּן	therefore

Causal/Reason

אֲשֶׁר	because	עַל־אֲשֶׁר	because
יַעַן	because	עַל־כִּי	because
כִּי	because	תַּחַת	because
מֵאֲשֶׁר	because		

Condition

אִם	if	כִּי	if
וְ	if/should	לוּ	if (irreal)

Concession

אִם	unless	כִּי־אִם	unless

כִּי   though   עַל   though, despite the fact

Modal Conjunctions (How)

Agency or *means*

בְּ   by

בְּיַד   by

Comparison

(כְּ) . . . כְּ   as, like

כְּ . . . כֵּן   as . . . so, just as . . . so

כַּאֲשֶׁר   as

Example

וְ   that is, for example (epexegetical *vav*)

Emphatic Conjunctions

אֲבָל   surely   גַּם   indeed

אַךְ   assuredly   הִנֵּה   indeed

אָמְנָה   truly

35

NOMINAL

We can use the label NOMINAL to refer to any word that does not function as a verb in a clause. A nominal may be

➤ a noun/substantive;

➤ pronoun;

➤ an adjective;

➤ a participle;

➤ infinitive (when not used as a verb);

➤ a preposition.

NOUN

A **NOUN** is a word that names something.

ENGLISH

Here are some classifications that nouns name.

> person   David, Moses, Miriam, father, sister

> place   town, country, Israel, Philistia, Ammon

> animal   donkey, fish, Leviathan

> thing   house, gate, road, Sabbath

> activity   running, birth, death

> idea or concept   truth, peace, righteousness

> quality   beauty

A **COMMON NOUN** is one that does not state the *name* of a *specific* person, place, etc. In English, a common noun begins with a lower case letter, unless, of course, it starts a sentence. In the list above, all nouns that are lower case are common nouns. Some use the label **SUBSTANTIVE** for this type of word.

A **PROPER NOUN** is one that states the *name* of a *specific* person, etc. In English, this type of noun is capitalized. In the list above, all nouns with capital letters are proper nouns.

A **COMPOUND NOUN** is made up of more than one word: *ice cream, Jordan Rift*.

BIBLICAL HEBREW

Nouns generally have the same function in Biblical Hebrew as they do in English. Since capitalization is not a phenomenon in Biblical Hebrew, common and proper nouns are not distinguished in writing. We need to keep track of certain things associated with nouns in Biblical Hebrew.

> gender (see **GENDER**, p. 25)

➢ number (see **Number**, p. 27)

➢ function: a noun can have a range of functions in clauses: subject (see **Subject**, p. 126), direct object of a verb (see **Direct/Objective Accusative**, p. 135, under the chapter **Predicate/Predication**), object of a preposition (see **Prepositional Phrases [PP]**, p. 141, under the chapter **Predicate/Predication**), etc.

PRONOUN

A **PRONOUN** is a classification of words we can use as a substitute for a noun (see **NOUN**, p. 37) or noun phrase. It can refer, therefore, to a person, place, animal, thing, activity, idea or concept, etc.

Rather than repeating the proper noun *Abraham* in the following two sentences,

> Abraham left Ur.
>
> Abraham went to Haran.

we can replace the second occurrence of *Abraham* with a pronoun.

> Abraham left Ur.
>
> *He* went to Haran.

Commonly we use a pronoun only after we have first mentioned the noun to which the pronoun will refer. The noun that the pronoun replaces is known as the **REFERENT** or **ANTECEDENT**. In our examples above, the referent of the pronoun *he* is the noun *Abraham*.

ENGLISH

We have several types of pronouns in English, the most important of which follow.

PERSONAL PRONOUN

These pronouns refer to different persons. They change their form depending on their function in a clause.

➢ **SUBJECT PERSONAL PRONOUN**: Personal pronouns can be used as the subject of a verb (see **SUBJECT**, p. 126).

> *I* talked, and *you* listened.
>> *Who* talked? *I* = subject
>>
>> *I* is the subject of the verb *talked*

Who listened? *You* = subject

You is the subject of *listened*

	Singular	**Plural**
1st person	I (common) — the person speaking	we (common) — the person speaking + others
2d person	you (common) — the person spoken to	you (common) — the persons spoken to
3d person	he (masculine) — she (feminine) — it (neuter) — the entity spoken about	they (common) — the entities spoken about

➤ **OBJECT PERSONAL PRONOUN:** Personal pronouns can be used as the object of a verb.

The king saw *him* but spoke to *us*.

The king saw *whom? him* = object

him is the object of the verb *saw*

The king spoke *to whom? us* = object of preposition

us is the object of the preposition *to*

	Singular	Plural
1st person	me (common) the person speaking	us (common) the person speaking + others
2d person	you (common) the person spoken to	you (common) the persons spoken to
3d person	him (masculine) her (feminine) it (neuter) the entity spoken about	them (common) the entities spoken about

POSSESSIVE PRONOUN

These pronouns replace a noun and specify the *possessor* of the replaced noun. The replacement of a noun is what distinguishes a possessive pronoun from a possessive adjective, which only modifies an existing noun (see **POSSESSIVE ADJECTIVE**, p. 61, under **ADJECTIVE**).

The king's horse is black. *His* is black.

The queen's horse is white. *Hers* is white.

	Singular	Plural
1st person	mine (common) the person speaking	ours (common) the person speaking + others
2d person	yours (common) the person spoken to	yours (common) the persons spoken to
3d person	his (masculine) hers (feminine) its (neuter) the entity spoken about	theirs (common) the entities spoken about

INTERROGATIVE PRONOUN

Interrogative pronouns replace a noun and introduce a question. We use different pronouns based on whether the replaced noun refers to something *animate* or something *inanimate*.

➢ ANIMATE

- **Who** takes the place of the subject of a verb.

    Who lives in the palace?
    └── subject

- **Whom** takes the place of the object of a verb or preposition (colloquial: American English speakers commonly use *who*, rather than *whom*, the "correct" form).

    Whom did you see in the palace? [Colloquial: *Who* did you see in the
    └── object of verb   palace?]

    To *whom* did you give the letter? [Colloquial: *Who* did you give the let-
    └── object of preposition   ter to?]

- **Whose** is used in questions of possession or ownership.

    Balaam found the donkey. *Whose* is it?

    Balaam has his donkey. *Whose* do you have?

➢ INANIMATE: **What** takes the place of a subject and object of a verb or preposition.

    What happened?
    └── subject

    What did you see in the palace?
    └── object of verb

    With *what* did you write the letter? [Colloquial: *What* did you write the letter
    └── object of preposition   with?]

42

DEMONSTRATIVE PRONOUN

These pronouns replace nouns and we categorize the pronouns according to whether they are **NEAR** (at hand) or **REMOTE** (farther away) and **SINGULAR** or **PLURAL**. English makes no distinction for gender. Do not confuse a demonstrative *pronoun* with a demonstrative *adjective* (see **DEMONSTRATIVE ADJECTIVE**, p. 63). The former *replaces* a noun while the latter modifies a noun usually by standing before the noun.

	Near	Remote
Singular	this	that
Plural	these	those

This is the ram.
　　　refers to the ram at hand (near)

These are the sheep on the hill.

That is the goat that lagged behind.

The stubborn ones are *those.*
　　　refers to stubborn ones farther away

(As a comparison, look at the following similar sentences, which use demonstrative *adjectives*.)

This ram belongs to him.
　　　modifies the noun *ram,*
　　　which is at hand (near)

These sheep pasture on the hill.

That goat lagged behind *those* men.

Those mules are stubborn.

REFLEXIVE PRONOUN

Reflexive pronouns refer back to the subject of a clause. They *reflect* the verb's process back to the subject.

Bathsheba bathed *herself.*

You built a house for *yourself.*

	Singular	Plural
1st person	myself (common) the person speaking	ourselves (common) the person speaking + others
2d person	yourself (common) the person spoken to	yourselves (common) the persons spoken to
3d person	himself (masculine) herself (feminine) itself (neuter) the entity spoken about	themselves (common) the entities spoken about

RELATIVE PRONOUN

These pronouns serve two primary functions.

1. They represent a previously mentioned noun or pronoun, which is known as the **REFERENT**, or **ANTECEDENT**, or **HEAD**. Each of the labels is truly inter-changeable. I shall settle on the first label for the following discussion.

    Eli saw the woman *who* cried in the courtyard.

    └── referent

2. They introduce a **RELATIVE CLAUSE**. A relative clause is a type of depend-ent/subordinate clause. That is, it is a clause that does not stand on its own and must be linked to a previous clause, which may be a main clause or an-other dependent/subordinate clause (see **CLAUSE**, p. 123). A relative clause may be either **RESTRICTIVE** or **NON-RESTRICTIVE**, the discussion of which we shall explore later in this subsection.

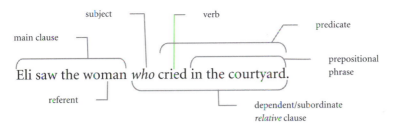

Who cried in the courtyard is not a free-standing clause. In this particular sentence *who* is a relative pronoun introducing the relative clause.

The form of the relative pronoun depends on (1) its syntactic function within the relative clause and (2) whether the referent is animate or inanimate. A relative pronoun may function within the relative clause as:

- a subject;

- an object of a verb or preposition;

- a possessive.

➢ **SUBJECT** OF A RELATIVE CLAUSE

The relative pronoun is different depending on whether the referent is animate or inanimate.

- animate referent ⇨ *who*

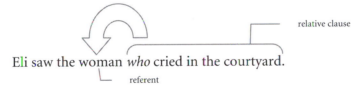

Who is the subject of the verb *cried.*

- inanimate referent ⇨ *which* or *that*

Ehud ran from Eglon's palace, *which* was in Moab.

Which is the subject of the verb *was.*

45

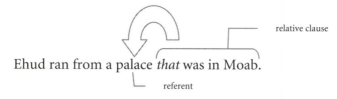

Ehud ran from a palace *that* was in Moab.

That is the subject of the verb *was*.

➢ **OBJECT OF A VERB OR PREPOSITION** WITHIN A RELATIVE CLAUSE

The relative pronoun is different depending on whether the referent is animate or inanimate. English speakers commonly omit relative pronouns when they function as objects of verbs or prepositions within relative clauses. I have placed them within parentheses.

- animate referent ⇨ *whom*

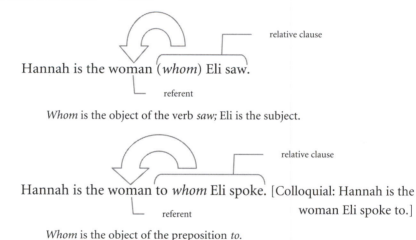

Hannah is the woman (*whom*) Eli saw.

Whom is the object of the verb *saw*; Eli is the subject.

Hannah is the woman to *whom* Eli spoke. [Colloquial: Hannah is the woman Eli spoke to.]

Whom is the object of the preposition *to*.

- inanimate referent ⇨ *which* or *that*

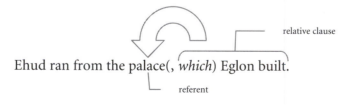

Ehud ran from the palace(, *which*) Eglon built.

Which is the object of the verb *built*; Eglon is the subject.

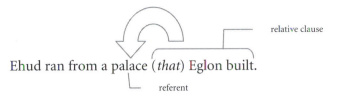

Ehud ran from a palace (*that*) Eglon built.

That is the object of the verb *built*; Eglon is the subject.

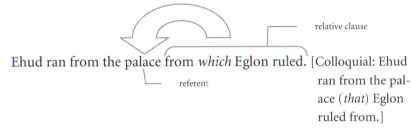

Ehud ran from the palace from *which* Eglon ruled. [Colloquial: Ehud ran from the palace (*that*) Eglon ruled from.]

Which is the object of the preposition *from*.

➢ **POSSESSIVE** WITHIN A RELATIVE CLAUSE

The possessive modifier **whose** is a relative pronoun. Its form does not change regardless of its function or referent.

These are the people *whose* houses Sennacherib destroyed.

➢ **RESTRICTIVE** VERSUS **NON-RESTRICTIVE** RELATIVE CLAUSES

A **RESTRICTIVE** relative clause *restricts* or *limits* the referent. Such a clause is essential to helping the reader or hearer understand the identity of the referent. In English these clauses do *not* use commas to set them off from the rest of the sentence. They are introduced by *who, whom, which,* or *that*.

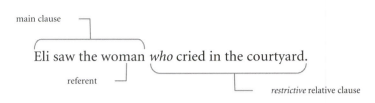

The relative clause here is essential in identifying the referent, *the woman*. Envision a situation in which there may be many women. This relative clause restricts the referent to one particular woman crying in the courtyard whom Eli saw.

A **NON-RESTRICTIVE** relative clause does *not* restrict or limit the referent. The referent is already clearly known. Such clauses simply offer more known information about an referent. In English these clauses do use commas to set them off from the rest of the sentence. They are introduced by *who, whom, which,* or *that*.

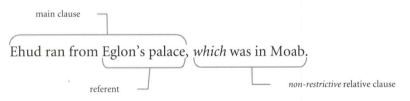

The relative clause here is not essential in identifying the referent, *Eglon's palace*. The clause is merely giving more known information about *Eglon's palace*. One already knows that Eglon's palace sits in Moab. The clause is non-restrictive.

BIBLICAL HEBREW

PERSONAL PRONOUN

These pronouns refer to different persons. They change their form depending on their function in a clause. In Hebrew, we make an important distinction between **INDEPENDENT** and **SUFFIXED** pronouns, also known as **PRONOMINAL** suffixes.

➢ **SUBJECT PERSONAL PRONOUN:** *Independent* personal pronouns can be used as the subject in a clause (see **SUBJECT**, p. 126).

אֲנַחְנוּ מֵחָרָן   *We* are from Haran.

we from-Haran   Genesis 29:4

Here are the forms of the independent personal pronouns:

	Singular	Plural
1st person	אֲנִי/אָנֹכִי (common)	אֲנַ֫חְנוּ (common)
	the person speaking	the person speaking + others
2d person	אַתָּ/אַתָּה (masculine)	אַתֶּם (masculine)
	אַתְּ (feminine)	אַתֶּן/אַתֵּ֫נָה (feminine)
	the person spoken to	the persons spoken to
3d person	הוּא (masculine)	הֵם/הֵ֫מָּה (masculine)
	הִיא (feminine)	הֵ֫נָּה (feminine)
	the entity spoken about	the entities spoken about

➢ **OBJECT PERSONAL PRONOUN:** Personal pronouns can be used as the object of a verb or preposition. Hebrew uses *suffixed* pronouns.

- object of a verb

  When a pronoun is the object of a verb, a pronominal suffix is added either (1) to the so-called direct object marker, אֵת/אֶת or (2) to the verb directly.

אֱלֹהִים	אֹתָם	וַיְבָ֫רֶךְ	God blessed *them.*
God	DO-*them*(mp)	and-he-blessed	Genesis 1:28

סְבָב֫וּנִי			They surround *me.*
they-surround-*me*			Psalm 109:3

  The forms of pronominal suffixes added to the so-called direct object marker are quite straightforward.

- object of a preposition

  When a pronoun is the object of a preposition, a pronominal suffix is added directly to the preposition.

אֱלֹהִים	לָהֶם	וַיֹּ֫אמֶר	God said to *them.* . . .
God	to-*them*	and-he-said	Genesis 1:28

The combinations of pronominal suffixes on the so-called direct object marker, on verbs, and on prepositions produce a great deal of variance. No single chart can capture them all without likely being too complicated to be of significant help. You should consult your grammar book as you go through the year of learning. The following chart, however, cites the range of the forms of the suffixed pronouns.

	Singular	**Plural**
1st person	יִ , נִי (common) the person speaking	נוּ (common) the person speaking + others
2d person	ךָ (masculine) ךְ (feminine) the person spoken to	כֶם (masculine) כֶן (feminine) the persons spoken to
3d person	הוּ, הָ , וֹ, וֹ (masculine) הָ, הָ (feminine) the entity spoken about	הֶם, הֶ (masculine) הֶן, הֶ (feminine) the entities spoken about

POSSESSIVE PRONOUN

These pronouns replace a noun and specify the *possessor* of the replaced noun. The replacement of a noun is what distinguishes a possessive pronoun from a possessive adjective, which only modifies an existing noun (see under **POSSESSIVE ADJECTIVE**, p. 61, 67). In Hebrew, possessive pronouns are suffixed on the possessed nouns.

בְּרִיתִי

covenant-*my*

my covenant

Genesis 9:9

אִשְׁתּוֹ

wife-*his*

his wife

Genesis 2:25

The combinations of possessive pronominal suffixes on nouns produce a lot of variety. You should consult your grammar book. The following chart, however, cites the range of the forms of the suffixed pronouns. The chart is the same as the one for personal pronouns, with one exception. The 1st person singular form נִי is not used as a possessive pronoun.

	Singular	**Plural**
1st person	ִי (common) the person speaking	נוּ (common) the person speaking + others
2d person	ךָ (masculine) ךְ (feminine) the person spoken to	כֶם (masculine) כֶן (feminine) the persons spoken to
3d person	וֹ, ה ָ, ו, וֹהוּ (masculine) הָ, ִהָ (feminine) the entity spoken about	הֶם, ם ָ (masculine) הֶן, ן ָ (feminine) the entities spoken about

INTERROGATIVE PRONOUN

These pronouns replace a noun and introduce a question. Biblical Hebrew, like English, uses different pronouns based on whether the replaced noun refers to something *animate* or something *inanimate*.

➤ ANIMATE: one pronoun, מִי, takes the place of a subject of a verb, object of a verb or preposition, and is used in questions of possession or ownership.

- **subject** of a verb

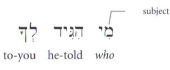

מִי   הִגִּיד   לְךָ
to-you   he-told   *who*

Who told you?

Genesis 3:11

- **object** of a verb or preposition

אֶת־מִי   אֶשְׁלַח
I-shall-send   DO-*whom*

Whom shall I send?

Isaiah 6:8

לְמִי־ אַתָּה   object of preposition

you   to-*whom*

To whom do you belong?

Genesis 32:18

- questions of possession or ownership

מִי אַתְּ בַּת־

you   *whom*   daughter-of

Whose daughter are you?

Genesis 24:23

➤ INANIMATE: one pronoun, מָה, with a variety of vocalizations, takes the place of a subject of a verb and an object of a verb or preposition.

- **subject** of a verb

מַה־ פִּשְׁעִי   subject

crime-my   *what*

What is my crime?

Genesis 31:36

- **object** of a verb or preposition

מֶה עָשִׂיתָ   object of verb

you-did   *what*

What have you done?

Genesis 4:10

בַּמָּה אֵדַע   object of preposition

I-shall-know   by-*what*

By what shall I know?

Genesis 15:8

Consult your grammar book for the various vocalizations of this particular pronoun.

DEMONSTRATIVE PRONOUN

Like English, these pronouns replace nouns. Unlike English, however, Biblical Hebrew only has one set of demonstrative pronouns, which are both near and remote, and they denote gender. Again, do not confuse a demonstrative *pronoun* with a demonstrative *adjective* (see **DEMONSTRATIVE ADJECTIVE**, p. 67). The former *replaces* a noun while the latter modifies a noun usually by standing after the noun and being definite.

	Near/Remote
Singular	זֶה (masculine)
	זֹה, זוֹ, זֹאת (feminine)
Plural	אֵל, אֵלֶּה (common)

הַדָּבָר	זֶה	
the-word	this/that	

This/That is the word. . . .

Numbers 30:2

אֵצֶר	בְנֵי־	אֵלֶּה
Ezer	sons-of	these

These/Those are Ezer's sons: . . .

Genesis 36:27

REFLEXIVE PRONOUN

Biblical Hebrew does not use reflexive pronouns. Reflexivity is conveyed through certain Stems (for example, Nifal and Hitpael).

RELATIVE PRONOUN

We commonly talk of Biblical Hebrew's relative pronouns being used for two types of relative clauses: (1) the **DEPENDENT** or **ATTRIBUTIVE RELATIVE CLAUSE**, which modifies a referent, and (2) the oddly labeled **INDEPENDENT RELATIVE CLAUSE**. The former is similar to how English's relative pronoun functions—it is linked to a previously mentioned noun or pronoun. The latter is independent and is not relative to another word or word-group around it.

The commonest relative pronoun is אֲשֶׁר. Another relative pronoun is -שֶׁ/-שַׁ plus doubling of the following consonant, where permissible. Yet another bundling is זֶה, זוֹ, and זֹה/זוֹ. Biblical Hebrew thus has three *primary* types of relative pronouns: (1) אֲשֶׁר, (2) the -שֶׁ type, and (3) the -זֹ type.

Unlike English, the form of the relative pronoun in Biblical Hebrew is *frozen*—it does not change regardless of its syntactic function within the relative clause or whether a referent/antecedent/head is animate or inanimate. Yes, the language has three primary forms—אֲשֶׁר, -שֶׁ, and -זֹ—but the choice of which form is used does not depend on its syntactic function or on animacy/inanimacy.

Let us look at the two types of relative clauses in turn.

Dependent or Attributive Relative Clause

As in English, the relative pronouns, when associated with dependent or attributive relative clauses, serve two primary functions.

1. They represent a previously mentioned noun or pronoun—the referent, antecedent, or head.

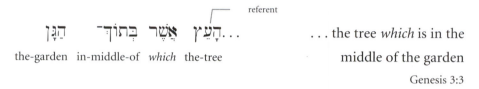

referent

... the tree *which* is in the middle of the garden

the-garden   in-middle-of   *which*   the-tree

Genesis 3:3

2. They introduce a **DEPENDENT** or **ATTRIBUTIVE RELATIVE CLAUSE**. This type of relative clause is a dependent/subordinate clause. That is, it is a clause that does not stand on its own and is linked to a previous clause, which may be a main clause or another dependent/subordinate clause (see **CLAUSE**, p. 123). Biblical Hebrew has no formal distinction between restrictive and non-restrictive relative clauses. No special punctuation or other written indicators convey the distinction that occurs in English.

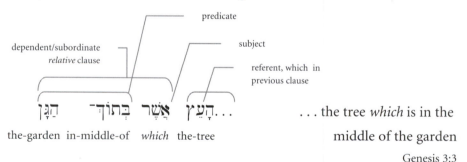

predicate

dependent/subordinate
relative clause

subject

referent, which in
previous clause

... the tree *which* is in the middle of the garden

the-garden   in-middle-of   *which*   the-tree

Genesis 3:3

אֲשֶׁר בְּתוֹךְ־הַגָּן is not a free-standing clause. In this particular sentence אֲשֶׁר is a relative pronoun introducing a dependent/attributive relative clause within the sentence.

A relative pronoun may function within the dependent/attributive relative clause as:

- a subject;

- an object of a verb or preposition;

- a possessive.

➤ **SUBJECT** OF A DEPENDENT/ATTRIBUTIVE RELATIVE CLAUSE

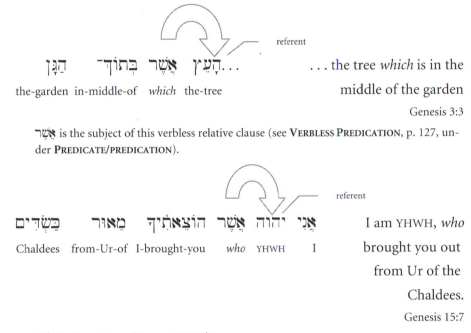

הַגָּן   בְּתוֹךְ־ אֲשֶׁר הָעֵץ...

the-garden in-middle-of *which* the-tree

referent

...the tree *which* is in the

middle of the garden

Genesis 3:3

אֲשֶׁר is the subject of this verbless relative clause (see **VERBLESS PREDICATION**, p. 127, under **PREDICATE/PREDICATION**).

כַּשְׂדִּים   מֵאוּר הוֹצֵאתִיךָ אֲשֶׁר יהוה אֲנִי

Chaldees from-Ur-of I-brought-you *who* YHWH   I

referent

I am YHWH, *who*

brought you out

from Ur of the

Chaldees.

Genesis 15:7

אֲשֶׁר is the subject of the verb הוֹצֵאתִי.

➤ **OBJECT OF A VERB OR PREPOSITION** WITHIN A DEPENDENT/ATTRIBUTIVE RELATIVE CLAUSE

Biblical Hebrew quite commonly places a **RESUMPTIVE PRONOUN** within the relative clause. This clearly specifies the syntactic function of the relative pronoun.

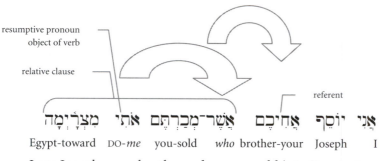

אֲנִי יוֹסֵף אֲחִיכֶם אֲשֶׁר־מְכַרְתֶּם אֹתִי מִצְרָיְמָה

Egypt-toward   DO-*me*   you-sold   *who*   brother-your   Joseph   I

I am Joseph, your brother, *whom* you sold into Egypt. Genesis 45:4

The resumptive pronoun, אֹתִי, is here the direct object within the relative clause. It is the *resumption* of the relative pronoun, אֲשֶׁר. This clearly shows that אֲשֶׁר is the object of the verb מְכַרְתֶּם. אֲשֶׁר refers back to אֲחִיכֶם, which is in the main clause and of course is animate, but that makes no difference in Biblical Hebrew.

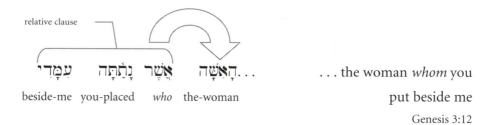

הָאִשָּׁה אֲשֶׁר נָתַתָּה עִמָּדִי ...

beside-me   you-placed   *who*   the-woman

... the woman *whom* you

put beside me

Genesis 3:12

No resumptive pronoun occurs in this relative clause. אֲשֶׁר is the object of the verb נָתַתָּה.

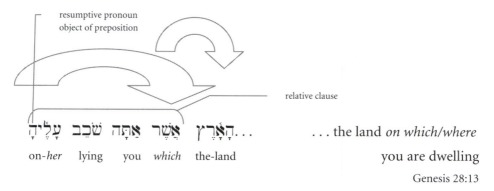

הָאָרֶץ אֲשֶׁר אַתָּה שֹׁכֵב עָלֶיהָ ...

on-*her*   lying   you   *which*   the-land

... the land *on which/where*

you are dwelling

Genesis 28:13

The resumptive pronoun הָ- is the object of the preposition, thus עָלֶיהָ. The pronoun is the *resumption* of the relative pronoun, אֲשֶׁר. This clearly shows that אֲשֶׁר is the object of the preposition. אֲשֶׁר refers back to הָאָרֶץ. Notice that הָאָרֶץ is a feminine, singular noun.

56

This is why the resumptive pronoun is 3fs, it must agree in gender and number with the noun to which it ultimately is referring.

➢ **POSSESSIVE** WITHIN A DEPENDENT/ATTRIBUTIVE RELATIVE CLAUSE

Possession is commonly shown through a **RESUMPTIVE PRONOUN.**

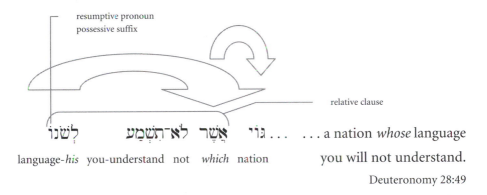

resumptive pronoun
possessive suffix

relative clause

לְשֹׁנוֹ   אֲשֶׁר לֹא־תִשְׁמַע   גּוֹי ...   ... a nation *whose* language

language-*his* you-understand not   *which* nation   you will not understand.

Deuteronomy 28:49

The resumptive pronoun וֹ- conveys possession, *his* language. We can call it a pronominal possessive suffix. The pronominal suffix is the *resumption* of the relative pronoun, אֲשֶׁר. This shows that אֲשֶׁר is the possessor of the language. אֲשֶׁר refers back to גּוֹי. Notice that גּוֹי is a masculine, singular noun. This is why the resumptive pronoun is 3ms, it must agree in gender and number with the noun to which it ultimately is referring.

Independent Relative Clause

The oddly-labeled independent relative clause is a clause that is not *relative* to another word or word-group around it. The whole clause, including the relative pronoun, can function as a basic syntactic element of a main clause—as a subject (see **SUBJECT**, p. 126), for example, or as an adverbial (see under **VERBAL PREDICATION**, p. 134, under **PREDICATE/PREDICATION**). It can be part of a construct chain or the object of a preposition.

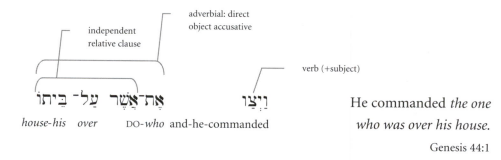

He commanded *the one
who was over his house.*

Genesis 44:1

Here the independent relative clause, אֲשֶׁר עַל־בֵּיתוֹ, functions as the **ADVERBIAL**, specifically, the **DIRECT OBJECT ACCUSATIVE** of the verb. This particular relative clause is so "independent," in fact, that it likely refers to a person's title within the royal household: *One who is over (the) house* or, simply, the *steward.* We could offer this translation: "He commanded his steward."

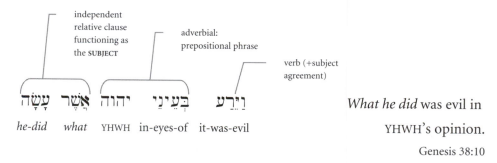

What he did was evil in
YHWH's opinion.

Genesis 38:10

ADJECTIVE

An **ADJECTIVE** is a word that modifies or describes a noun or a pronoun. We generally classify them according to how they describe a noun or pronoun. Adjectives are **ADNOMINAL** phenomena, that is, they are most closely linked *to nouns,* precisely what *ad-nominal* means. As a contrast, adverbs are most closely linked to verbs, *ad-verb.*

ENGLISH

The main types of adjectives we see in English are: (1) descriptive, (2) possessive, (3) interrogative, and (4) demonstrative.

DESCRIPTIVE ADJECTIVE

A descriptive adjective describes a characteristic or quality. It answers the question *what kind?* This type of adjective may be an **ATTRIBUTIVE** or a **PREDICATE** adjective. It may also function as a noun itself—a **SUBSTANTIVE** adjective. Descriptive adjectives may *compare* a noun's attribute—a **COMPARATIVE** adjective—and convey the highest or lowest degree of an attribute—a **SUPERLATIVE** adjective.

➤ **ATTRIBUTIVE DESCRIPTIVE ADJECTIVE:** An attributive descriptive adjective *modifies* a noun often by preceding it.

> *true* prophet
>
> attributive descriptive adjective modifying *prophet*

> *false* prophet
>
> attributive descriptive adjective modifying *prophet*

➤ **PREDICATE DESCRIPTIVE ADJECTIVE:** A predicate descriptive adjective makes a *comment* about a noun or pronoun. It follows a linking verb, most commonly a form of *be,* though *seem, appear, become, feel,* and *taste* are frequent.

> The prophet's words were *true.*
>
> linking verb ⟶   predicate descriptive adjective asserting a comment about *the prophet's words*

He is *good.*

The mannah tastes *fine.*

linking verb — predicate descriptive adjective asserting a comment about *the mannah*

The Negev sun feels *hot.*

➢ **SUBSTANTIVE DESCRIPTIVE ADJECTIVE:** A substantive descriptive adjective is one that functions as a noun. It does not modify another noun but becomes a noun in function.

The *poor* live outside the city gate.

The *rich* live by the palace.

The king invited only the *wealthy.*

➢ **COMPARATIVE DESCRIPTIVE ADJECTIVE:** A comparative descriptive adjective conveys when nouns have a greater, lesser, or equal degree of an attribute. Here is how English conveys comparison.

- Comparison of greater degree

  ◆ short adjective + *-er* + *than* + noun whose attribute is surpassed

    Goliath is tall*er than* David.

    David is the noun with the surpassed attribute

    Goliath is the noun that possesses a greater degree of the attribute *tall*

    David is young*er than* Goliath.

  ◆ *more* + long(er) adjective + *than* + noun whose attribute is surpassed

    Goliath is *more* experienced *than* David.

- Comparison of lesser degree

  ◆ *not as* + adjective + *as* + noun whose attribute is unsurpassed

60

Saul is *not as* brave *as* David.

Saul is the noun that possesses a
lesser degree of the attribute *brave*

David is the noun with
the unsurpassed attribute

- ◆ *less* + adjective + *than*

    Israel's army is *less* experienced *than* the Philistine's.

- Comparison of equal degree

    - ◆ (*as* +) adjective + *as* + noun whose attribute is equaled

        Goliath is (*as*) tall *as* a tree.

Goliath is the noun that possesses
an equal degree of the attribute *tall*

tree is the noun with
the equaled attribute

➤ **SUPERLATIVE DESCRIPTIVE ADJECTIVE**: A superlative descriptive adjective conveys the highest or lowest degree of an attribute.

- Superlative of highest degree

    - ◆ *the* + short adjective + *-est*

        Goliath is *the* tall*est* among the champions.

    - ◆ *the most* + long(er) adjective

        Goliath is *the most* experienced among the champions.

- Superlative of lowest degree

    - ◆ *the least* + adjective

        David is *the least* experienced.

POSSESSIVE ADJECTIVE

A possessive adjective describes or modifies a noun by stating who possesses it. The owner is the **POSSESSOR** and the modified noun is the **POSSESSED**.

	Singular	**Plural**
1st person	my (common)	our (common)
2d person	your (common)	your (common)
3d person	his (masculine) her (feminine) its (neuter)	their (common)

A possessive adjective has only the possessor in mind, not the possessed. That is, it does not agree in gender or number with the possessed.

Jael's tentpeg is new.

        possessor

Her tentpeg is new.

        noun possessed

Solomon's wives lived at the palace.

        possessor

His wives lived at the palace.

        noun possessed

INTERROGATIVE ADJECTIVE

An interrogative adjective asks a question about a noun. *Which* and *what* are interrogative adjectives *when they are in front of the noun and ask a question.* The form never changes regardless of the syntactic function of the modified noun.

Which road leads to Ashqelon?

        modifies the subject *road*

From *which* town did you come?

        modifies *town*, the object of the preposition *from*

What vineyard do you want?

        modifies the object *vineyard*

DEMONSTRATIVE ADJECTIVE

A demonstrative adjective points out a noun. Think of the related word *demonstrate*. The demonstrative adjective *demonstrates,* points out. We categorize demonstrative adjectives according to whether they are NEAR (at hand) or REMOTE (farther away) and SINGULAR or PLURAL. English makes no distinction for gender.

	Near	Remote
Singular	this	that
Plural	these	those

This clay jar is Abigail's but *those* jars are Nabal's.

refers to one clay jar at hand   refers to many jars farther away

We make a clear distinction between demonstrative adjectives and demonstrative *pronouns* (see **DEMONSTRATIVE PRONOUN**, p. 43).

➤ Demonstrative adjectives stand before a noun and modify it.

> *This* ram belongs to him.
>
> *These* sheep pasture on the hill.
>
> *That* goat lagged behind *those* men.
>
> *Those* mules are stubborn.

➤ Demonstrative pronouns *replace* a noun and thus do not modify one.

> *This* is the ram.
>
> *These* are the sheep on the hill.
>
> *That* is the goat that lagged behind.
>
> The stubborn ones are *those*.

BIBLICAL HEBREW

DESCRIPTIVE ADJECTIVE

➢ **ATTRIBUTIVE DESCRIPTIVE ADJECTIVE:** An attributive descriptive adjective in Biblical Hebrew commonly follows the noun it modifies and agrees with the noun's *definiteness, gender,* and *number.*

attributive descriptive adjective modifying מֶלֶךְ, which is indefinite, masculine, and singular

מֶלֶךְ טוֹב

good   king

a *good* king

attributive descriptive adjective modifying הַמֶּלֶךְ, which is definite, masculine, and singular

הַמֶּלֶךְ הַטּוֹב

the-good   the-king

the *good* king

attributive descriptive adjective modifying שְׁמוֹ, which is definite (because of the 3ms suffix), masculine, and singular

שְׁמוֹ   הַגָּדוֹל

the-big   name-his

his *great* name

1 Samuel 12:22

attributive descriptive adjective modifying מְלָכוֹת, which is indefinite, feminine, and plural

מְלָכוֹת טוֹבוֹת

good   queens

good queens

➢ **PREDICATE DESCRIPTIVE ADJECTIVE:** A predicate descriptive adjective in Biblical Hebrew stands commonly as the predicate in a *verbless* clause (see **ADJECTIVE PREDICATE,** p. 128). It also can occur as part of the predicate in a *verbal* clause.

• **Verbless Clause:** A descriptive adjective that functions as a predicate in a verbless clause is *always indefinite.* The clause's subject is *definite.* The predicate adjective agrees with the subject, though, in gender and number. English supplies a form of *be,* commonly, or another linking verb, as we saw above. Biblical Hebrew, however, has no linking verb in this verbless construction. The predicate adjective in a verbless clause is simply side-by-side with the subject, that is, it is *juxtaposed.*

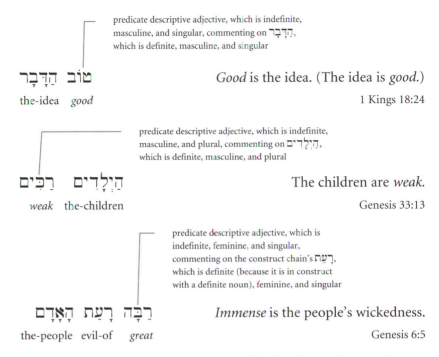

predicate descriptive adjective, which is indefinite, masculine, and singular, commenting on הַדָּבָר, which is definite, masculine, and singular

טוֹב הַדָּבָר

the-idea   good

Good is the idea. (The idea is *good*.)

1 Kings 18:24

predicate descriptive adjective, which is indefinite, masculine, and plural, commenting on הַיְלָדִים, which is definite, masculine, and plural

הַיְלָדִים רַכִּים

weak   the-children

The children are *weak*.

Genesis 33:13

predicate descriptive adjective, which is indefinite, feminine, and singular, commenting on the construct chain's רָעַת, which is definite (because it is in construct with a definite noun), feminine, and singular

רַבָּה רָעַת הָאָדָם

the-people   evil-of   great

Immense is the people's wickedness.

Genesis 6:5

- **Verbal Clause**: Descriptive adjectives in Biblical Hebrew do occur in verbal clauses, that is, where a verb is present and an adjective is part of the predicate. The verb is commonly a form of הָיָה *to be*.

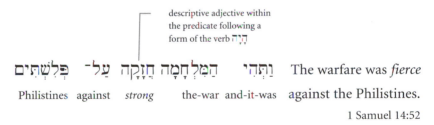

descriptive adjective within the predicate following a form of the verb הָיָה

וַתְּהִי הַמִּלְחָמָה חֲזָקָה עַל־ פְּלִשְׁתִּים

Philistines   against   *strong*   the-war   and-it-was

The warfare was *fierce* against the Philistines.

1 Samuel 14:52

➢ **SUBSTANTIVE DESCRIPTIVE ADJECTIVE**: Like English, a substantive descriptive adjective in Biblical Hebrew is one that functions as a noun.

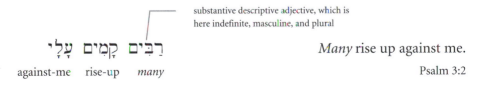

substantive descriptive adjective, which is here indefinite, masculine, and plural

רַבִּים קָמִים עָלָי

against-me   rise-up   *many*

Many rise up against me.

Psalm 3:2

65

substantive descriptive adjective, which is
here definite, feminine, and singular

יָפָה   כַּלְּבָנָה

like-the-*white(-one)* beautiful

beautiful as the *moon (white one)*

Song of Songs 6:10

➤ **COMPARATIVE DESCRIPTIVE ADJECTIVE:** Biblical Hebrew has no special form
of the adjective itself when it conveys comparison. It also has no word
equivalent to English's use of *more* or *less.* Biblical Hebrew has comparison of
greater and equal degree.

- Comparison of greater degree

  ◆ מִן prefixes to the noun or pronoun whose attribute is surpassed. The
    adjective conveys the attribute.

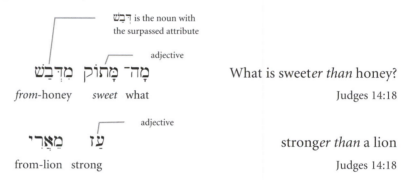

דְּבַשׁ is the noun with
the surpassed attribute

adjective

מַה־ מָּתוֹק מִדְּבַשׁ

from-honey   *sweet* what

What is sweet*er than* honey?

Judges 14:18

adjective

עַז   מֵאֲרִי

from-lion strong

strong*er than* a lion

Judges 14:18

- Comparison of equal degree

  ◆ כְּ is used in expressions with a descriptive adjective.

predicate descriptive
adjective

שְׁחוֹרָה אֲנִי . . . כְּאָהֳלֵי   קֵדָר

Qedar *like*-tents-of . . . I   dark

Dark am I . . .

like the tents of Qedar.

Song of Songs 1:5

➤ **SUPERLATIVE DESCRIPTIVE ADJECTIVE:** Biblical Hebrew has no special form
for the adjective itself when the superlative is conveyed. A variety of constructions, however, convey the superlative.

- Superlative of highest degree

  - an adjective definite either with an article or in a definite construct chain

הַקָּטֹן the-small [one]	the *smallest/youngest* [son] Genesis 42:13
בָּנָיו קְטֹן sons-his small-of	the *smallest/youngest* of his sons 2 Chronicles 21:17

  - adjective + the preposition בְּ prefixed to a plural noun

בַּנָּשִׁים הַיָּפָה among-the-women the-beautiful [one]	the *most beautiful* among women Song of Songs 1:8

Biblical Hebrew also conveys the superlative without the use of adjectives. It often uses the construct chain and מִן + כֹל . Consult your grammar textbook.

POSSESSIVE ADJECTIVE

Biblical Hebrew does not have possessive adjectives. Nouns convey possession through suffixes added on the end of the possessed noun. Consult your grammar textbook for the forms.

INTERROGATIVE ADJECTIVE

Biblical Hebrew has no formal interrogative adjective. Later dialects will develop one from the type of construction we see in 2 Kings 3:8.

אֵי־ זֶה הַדֶּרֶךְ נַעֲלֶה we-shall-go-up the-road *this* *where* (=where is this, the road we shall ascend?)	*Which* road shall we ascend?

DEMONSTRATIVE ADJECTIVE

We categorize demonstrative adjectives in Biblical Hebrew, like English, according to whether they are NEAR (at hand) or REMOTE (farther away) and SINGULAR or PLURAL. Gender is distinguished, unlike English.

	Near	**Remote**
Singular	זֶה (masculine) זֹה, זוֹ, זֹאת (feminine)	הוּא (masculine) הִיא (feminine)
Plural	אֵל, אֵלֶּה (common)	הֵם, הֵמָּה (masculine) הֵנָּה (feminine)

The remote demonstrative adjectives are actually the 3d person independent pronouns (see **SUBJECT PERSONAL PRONOUN**, p. 48). Those pronouns take on the additional function of a remote demonstrative adjective.

Biblical Hebrew also makes a clear distinction between demonstrative adjectives and demonstrative *pronouns* (see **DEMONSTRATIVE PRONOUN**, p. 52).

➢ Demonstrative adjectives *follow* a definite noun and are themselves *definite,* that is, they have a definite article.

הָאִישׁ הַזֶּה

the-this the-man

this man

הָאִשָּׁה הַזֹּאת

the-this the-woman

this woman

הָאֲנָשִׁים הָאֵלֶּה

the-these the-men

these men

הַנָּשִׁים הָאֵלֶּה

the-these the-women

these women

➢ Demonstrative pronouns *replace* a noun and thus do not modify one.

זֶה הָאִישׁ

the-man *this*

This is the man.

זֹאת הָאִשָּׁה

the-woman *this*

This is the woman.

ADVERB

An **ADVERB** is commonly a word that modifies or describes a verb, an adjective, or another adverb. Adverbs convey such concepts as time, place, quantity, manner, and intensity.

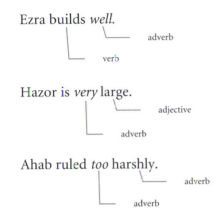

Ezra builds *well.*

Hazor is *very* large.

Ahab ruled *too* harshly.

An **ADVERB** or **ADVERBIAL** can also refer to all components of language connected to the verb. This is a broad use of the term, and usually *ADVERBIAL* is the preferred label for this wide use. I explore this in detail under the chapter **PREDICATE/PREDICATION**, particularly under **VERBAL PREDICATION**, p. 134.

ENGLISH

➤ adverbs of **TIME** address the issue of *when?*

The orphans arrived *early.*

The Midianite caravan started *late.*

➤ adverbs of **PLACE** address the issue of *where?*

The orphans were left *behind.*

Lot looked *around.*

➤ adverbs of **QUANTITY** address the issue *how much?* or *how well?*

The top of Mt. Hermon is *very* cold.

Sarah eats *little*.

➤ adverbs of **MANNER** address the issue of *how?*

They walked along the path *carefully*.

The daughters of Jerusalem danced *beautifully*.

➤ adverbs of **INTENSITY** address emphasis

Solomon was a *really* wise king.

Jonathan did not *actually* hate Saul, his father.

➤ adverbs of **CAUSE** or **PURPOSE** address the issue of *why? what for?*

I will *therefore* refuse to pay Sennacherib!

Some adverbs in English are precisely the same form as their adjective counterpart. Remember that adverbs modify verbs, adjectives, and other adverbs, while adjectives modify nouns and pronouns.

Adverb	Adjective
The chariot drove *fast*.	The *fast* charioteer won the battle.
I *only* drink water from the Jordan.	Jerusalem was the *only* city left standing.
They work *hard*.	That was *hard* work.

BIBLICAL HEBREW

We commonly talk about adverbs in Biblical Hebrew being *primitive, derived,* or *other parts of speech.*

➤ primitive adverbs

לֹא־תַעֲשֶׂה כָל־מְלָאכָה   You must *not/never* do any work.

work any you-will-do *not*   Exodus 20:10

וַיָּ֫שֶׂם שָׁ֖ם אֶת־הָֽאָדָ֑ם

DO-the-man *there* and-he-placed

He placed the man *there*.

Genesis 2:8

➤ derived adverbs

derived from אָמֵן "faithfulness"

הַאַ֖ף אֻמְנָ֣ם אֵלֵ֑ד

I-can-give birth *verily* INTERROGATIVE-also

How can I *surely* give birth to a child?

Genesis 18:13

derived from יוֹם "day"

וַעֲנַ֨ן יהוה עֲלֵיהֶ֤ם יוֹמָ֔ם

by-day over-them YHWH and-cloud-of

The cloud of YHWH was over them *by day*.

Numbers 10:34

➤ other parts of speech used as adverbs

substantive meaning "unitedness" used as an adverb

וַיֵּאָסְפ֖וּ יַ֑חַד

and-they-were-assembled *together*

They assembled *together*.

2 Samuel 10:15

adjective used as an adverb; remember that English has the same phenomenon

מַלְאֲכֵ֣י שָׁל֔וֹם מַ֖ר יִבְכָּיֽוּן

messengers-of peace *bitter* they-cry

Ambassadors of peace are weeping *bitterly*.

Isaiah 33:7

infinitives absolute used as adverbs

וַיִּגַּ֥שׁ הַפְּלִשְׁתִּ֖י הַשְׁכֵּ֣ם וְהַעֲרֵ֑ב

and-he-neared the-Philistine *do-early-morning* and-*do-evening*

The Philistine approached *every morning and evening*.

1 Samuel 17:16

71

Broad Use of the Term Adverbial

I mentioned above that the term ADVERBIAL could refer to any component of language connected to the verb. Dividing adverbials into two main categories is helpful: (1) DIRECT/OBJECTIVE ACCUSATIVES and (2) ADVERBIAL MODIFIERS. I discuss this in detail under the section VERBAL PREDICATION (see p. 134) in the chapter PREDICATE/PREDICATION.

PARTICIPLE

A **PARTICIPLE** is a word form that *participates* in the world of the verb and the world of the nominal. It can function as though it were a verb and as an adjective.

ENGLISH

The participle in English has

➤ tense: *present* or *past* (see **TENSE**, p. 87);

➤ voice: *active* or *passive* (see **VOICE**, p. 116).

The **PRESENT PARTICIPLE** ends in *-ing*: eat*ing*, rid*ing*, writ*ing*.

The **PAST PARTICIPLE** is the form we use after **He has**: He has *eaten, ridden, written*. We form the past participle usually by adding *-ed, -d, -t*, or *-en* to the dictionary form of the verb.

Participles have a variety of functions in English.

➤ as a verbal form used in combination with an auxiliary verb to create several tenses (see **TENSE**, p. 87)

Present participle

Baruch *is writing* a report. = absolute present progressive

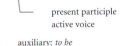
        present participle
        active voice
    auxiliary: *to be*

Baruch *was writing* a report. = absolute past progressive

        present participle
        active voice
    auxiliary: *to be*

Baruch *has been writing* a report. = present perfect progressive

     present participle
     active voice

    auxiliary: *to be*

  auxiliary: *to have*

Past participle

With the auxiliary verb *to have*, the past participle forms tense. With the auxiliary verb *to be*, the past participle assists in conveying the passive voice.

Baruch *has written* a report. = present perfect (active voice)

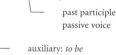

    past participle
    active voice

  auxiliary: *to have*

Baruch *had written* a report. = past perfect/pluperfect (active voice)

    past participle
    active voice

  auxiliary: *to have*

A report *was written* by Baruch. = passive voice

    past participle
    passive voice

  auxiliary: *to be*

➢ as adjectives

Attributive adjective (= a word is *modified* by an adjective)

Isaiah was an *amazing* prophet.

    present participle
    active voice
    modifies *prophet*

The *broken* pot was a nicely *burnished* piece.

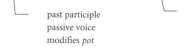

  past participle   past participle
  passive voice   passive voice
  modifies *pot*   modifies *piece*

Predicate adjective (= an adjective makes a *comment* on a word with the help of a linking verb)

Isaiah was *amazing*.

> present participle
> active voice
> makes a comment about *Isaiah*

linking verb

Substantive adjective (= an adjective functions as a noun)

The *amazed* left Sinai.

> past participle
> active voice
> functioning as a noun

➤ beginning a participial phrase (The phrase, which by definition has no subject, modifies a word outside the phrase.)

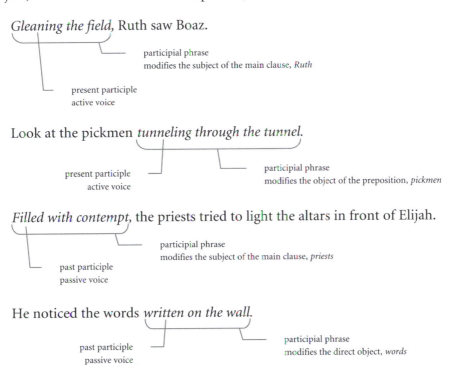

Gleaning the field, Ruth saw Boaz.

> participial phrase
> modifies the subject of the main clause, *Ruth*

present participle
active voice

Look at the pickmen *tunneling through the tunnel*.

present participle
active voice

> participial phrase
> modifies the object of the preposition, *pickmen*

Filled with contempt, the priests tried to light the altars in front of Elijah.

> participial phrase
> modifies the subject of the main clause, *priests*

past participle
passive voice

He noticed the words *written on the wall*.

past participle
passive voice

> participial phrase
> modifies the direct object, *words*

75

BIBLICAL HEBREW

The participle in Biblical Hebrew has voice: *active* or *passive* (see **VOICE**, p. 116).

Unlike English, however, Biblical Hebrew does *not* have tense.

Technically, only in the Qal Stem can we talk about active and passive participles. The passive derived stems in Biblical Hebrew (Nifal, Pual, Hofal) have participles that convey the passive, of course, but they do not have *active* participles. They have simply a Nifal, or a Pual, or a Hofal participle. We shall focus primarily on the Qal Stem.

The participle focuses more on the *participant* related to the verbal process associated with the participle. This, in part, explains why a participle inflects for the number and gender of words to which it is closely connected. The other non-finite verb form in Biblical Hebrew, the **INFINITIVE** (p. 80), focuses more on the *process* and thus rarely is marked for number and gender—possessive suffixes being the only indicator of number and gender related to the infinitive's verbal process.

The Qal Stem has the following participles:

➢ active;

- fientive (ms קֹטֵל, the *qōtēl* pattern) (for *fientive* see **VERB**, p. 84)

- stative (ms קָטֵל)

➢ passive (ms קָטוּל).

The participle in Biblical Hebrew may function as (1) a substantive, (2) an adjective, (3) a relative, and (4) a predicate.

SUBSTANTIVAL FUNCTION

Participles can function as common nouns, that is, substantives.

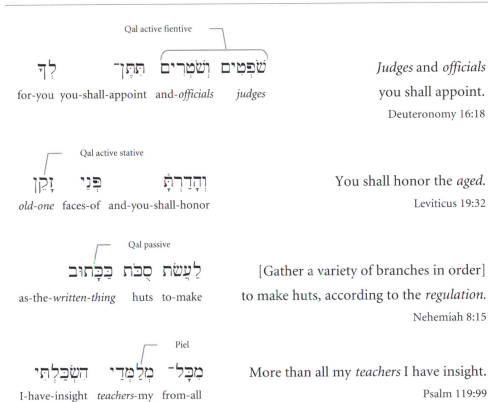

Qal active fientive

שֹׁפְטִים וְשֹׁטְרִים תִּתֶּן־ לְךָ
judges and-*officials* you-shall-appoint for-you

Judges and *officials*
you shall appoint.

Deuteronomy 16:18

Qal active stative

וְהָדַרְתָּ פְּנֵי זָקֵן
and-you-shall-honor faces-of old-one

You shall honor the *aged*.

Leviticus 19:32

Qal passive

לַעֲשֹׂת סֻכֹּת כַּכָּתוּב
to-make huts as-the-*written-thing*

[Gather a variety of branches in order]
to make huts, according to the *regulation*.

Nehemiah 8:15

Piel

מִכָּל־ מְלַמְּדַי הִשְׂכַּלְתִּי
from-all *teachers*-my I-have-insight

More than all my *teachers* I have insight.

Psalm 119:99

ADJECTIVAL FUNCTION

Participles in Biblical Hebrew can function as *attributive* and *predicate* adjectives (see under **ADJECTIVE**, p. 59).

Attributive Adjective

The participle may function in the same way as an attributive adjective. The participle commonly follows the noun it modifies and agrees with the noun's *definiteness, gender,* and *number.*

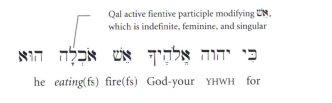

Qal active fientive participle modifying אֵשׁ,
which is indefinite, feminine, and singular

הוּא אֹכְלָה אֵשׁ אֱלֹהֶיךָ יהוה כִּי
he *eating*(fs) fire(fs) God-your YHWH for

As for YHWH your God,
a *consuming* fire is he.

Deuteronomy 4:24

77

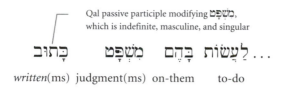

Qal passive participle modifying מִשְׁפָּט,
which is indefinite, masculine, and singular

כָּתוּב   מִשְׁפָּט   בָּהֶם   לַעֲשׂוֹת ...

written(ms) judgment(ms) on-them   to-do

... to execute on them

(the) *written* judgment

Psalm 149:9

Predicate Adjective

The *passive* participle (*not* the active participle) may function in the same way as a predicate adjective. The passive participle used as a predicate adjective conveys a *state of being,* not fientivity (activity or dynamism). (If fientivity is conveyed in the passive participle, the participle is then functioning as a *predicate,* that is, as a predicator; see p. 79 under **Predicate Function**.) The predicate adjective function of the passive participle agrees with the subject in gender and number and is simply side-by-side with the subject, that is, it is juxtaposed. The participle is indefinite while the clause's subject is definite.

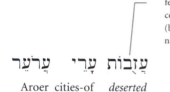

Qal passive participle, which is *in*definite,
feminine, and plural, commenting on the
construct chain's עָרֵי, which is definite
(because it is in construct with a geographical
name), feminine, and plural

עֲזֻבוֹת עָרֵי עֲרֹעֵר

Aroer cities-of *deserted*

Deserted are the cities of Aroer.

Isaiah 17:2

The example is describing a state of being: the cities lie in a deserted state.

RELATIVE FUNCTION

The participle can function as the equivalent of a relative clause. This *relative participle* is commonly definite.

Qal active fientive participle, which
is definite, feminine, and plural

אֶת כָּל־אֲשֶׁר עָשָׂה   הָרֹאֹת   עֵינֶיךָ

he-did which all DO *the-ones-which-saw* eyes-your

Your eyes are *the ones*

that saw all he did.

Deuteronomy 3:21

עַל־הַמִּזְבֵּחַ הַבָּנוּי

the-built   the-altar   on

upon the altar *which had been built*

Judges 6:28

PREDICATE FUNCTION

A participle is commonly used as a predicator in a *verbless* clause. Though a *predicate participle* in Biblical Hebrew seems to approximate the *function* of a finite verb, a clause with a predicate participle is nevertheless considered verbless. This use of the participle does not formally convey aspect/tense and mood, which is what a finite verb, by definition, does. The finite verbal forms in the context surrounding a predicate participle inform us of where to root the participle in terms of aspect/time and mood.

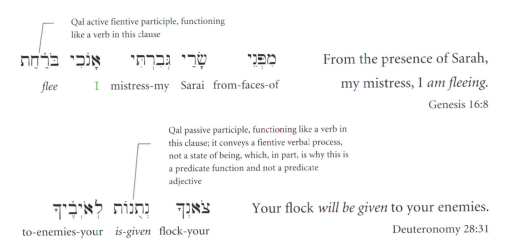

מִפְּנֵי שָׂרִי גְּבִרְתִּי אָנֹכִי בֹּרַחַת

flee   I   mistress-my   Sarai   from-faces-of

From the presence of Sarah, my mistress, I *am fleeing.*

Genesis 16:8

צֹאנְךָ נְתֻנוֹת לְאֹיְבֶיךָ

to-enemies-your   *is-given*   flock-your

Your flock *will be given* to your enemies.

Deuteronomy 28:31

The last example may have you asking yourself how a passive participle's function as a predicate adjective is different from its function as a predicate or verb. The distinction is that the former conveys a *state of being* or a *result.* The latter conveys a fientivity (activity, dynamism) in the passive voice, precisely what this last example expresses.

INFINITIVE

An **INFINITIVE** is a verbal noun (part verb, part noun) and a non-finite verb form (for a definition see **FINITE AND NON-FINITE**, p. 84, under **VERB**). It focuses on the *process* involved with the verb. In many languages, the infinitive is the *base* or *dictionary* form.

ENGLISH

The infinitive is the dictionary form of the verb: *walk, see, read,* etc. The infinitive is often used along with the main verb. We commonly attach **to** to the infinitive.

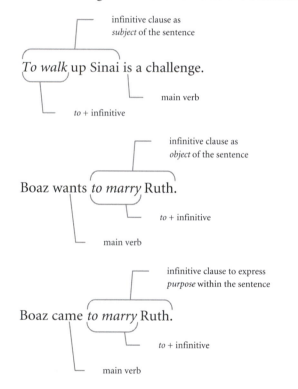

With some verbs, like *let* and *must,* we use the infinitive without *to.*

Elimelech must *do* his chores.

main verb — infinitive

BIBLICAL HEBREW

The infinitive in Biblical Hebrew is *not* the base or dictionary form. It is a specially marked form. Hebrew, in fact, has two types of infinitives: (1) INFINITIVE ABSOLUTE and (2) INFINITIVE CONSTRUCT. The other non-finite verb form, the PARTICIPLE, focuses more on the *participant* related to the verb. This, in part, explains why participles inflect for number and gender. Infinitives, which focus more on the verb *process,* are rarely so marked. The suffixes added to infinitives construct are the only indicators of gender and number associated with the verbal process.

Your primary textbook undoubtedly discusses the many functions of the infinitives absolute and construct. Consult it. You can also find more extensive discussions in reference grammars.

GERUND

A **GERUND** is a verbal noun (part verb, part noun) that functions as a noun in a clause.

ENGLISH

English forms gerunds by adding *-ing* to verbs. A gerund functions in a clause virtually in any way that a noun can. It can be the subject or an adverbial.

A gerund has the same form as a present participle (see under **PARTICIPLE**, p. 73). You must, therefore, be careful not to confuse the two:

➤ A word ending in *-ing* is a gerund if you are able to form a question by replacing that word with the interrogative *what*. A gerund answers the question.

Cooking can be fun.
    a noun from the verb *cook*
    subject of the clause

What can be fun? *Cooking* = gerund

Lot often thought about *moving*.
    a noun from the verb *move*
    object of the preposition *about* in the predicate

Lot often thought about *what? Moving* = gerund

➤ A word ending in *-ing* is a present participle if it fails the "gerund test." If you are forced to form a question by replacing the *-ing*-word with more than one word or you must use a form of the verb *do*, the word is a present participle.

Shepherding near Bethlehem, David fought a lion.
    present participle
    active voice

What was David *doing* near Bethlehem? *Shepherding* = present participle

BIBLICAL HEBREW

Biblical Hebrew has no gerund. The language's **INFINITIVE CONSTRUCT** and **INFINITIVE ABSOLUTE**, however, sometimes function as gerunds (see **INFINITIVE**, p. 80). The English translation of a Biblical Hebrew infinitive used as a gerund will not always meet the "gerund test."

An infinitive is functioning as a gerund if it:

➢ is NOT functioning as the *subject* of a sentence (see English example under **INFINITIVE**, p. 80);

➢ is NOT functioning as the *object* of a sentence (see English example under **INFINITIVE**, p. 80);

➢ is NOT expressing *purpose* or *result* (see English example under **INFINITIVE**, p. 80);

➢ but IS expressing another circumstance or motive.[5]

		ל + Piel infinitive construct + 3ms suffix		
לְקַדְּשׁוֹ	הַשַּׁבָּת	אֶת־יוֹם	שָׁמוֹר	Keep the Sabbath
to-sanctify-him	the-Sabbath	DO-day-of	keep	*by sanctifying it!*
				Deuteronomy 5:12

---

[5] For more detail, see Cynthia L. Miller, *The Representation of Speech in Biblical Hebrew Narrative: A Linguistic Analysis* (Harvard Semitic Museum Monographs 55; Atlanta: Scholars Press, 1996), 175–85.

VERB

A **VERB** is a word that conveys a process, whether full of action or static (for example, *seem* or *be*). In the chapter **SEMANTICS: PROCESSES, ROLES, AND CIRCUMSTANCES**, we talk about three primary spheres of verbal processes: the *material* = doing, the *mental* = sensing, and the *relational*. See that discussion, p. 143.

Here are some basic concepts closely associated with verbs.

➤ **FINITE AND NON-FINITE**

A verb is considered **FINITE** if it conveys *aspect/tense* and *mood*. In Biblical Hebrew the finite verbal forms are the Suffix (Perfect) and Prefix (Imperfect) Conjugations.

A verb is considered **NON-FINITE** if it does not convey aspect/tense and mood. In Biblical Hebrew the infinitives are truly non-finite verbal forms.

➤ **TRANSITIVE AND INTRANSITIVE**

A **TRANSITIVE** verb governs a direct object (direct object accusative). Such a verb tends to be fientive (see concept below).

The man *wrote* the letter.

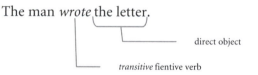

direct object

transitive fientive verb

An **INTRANSITIVE** verb does not govern a direct object.

The bees *swarm.*

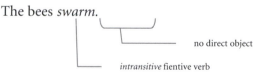

no direct object

intransitive fientive verb

➢ **FIENTIVE AND STATIVE**

A **FIENTIVE** verb conveys activity or a dynamic situation. The verb may be *transitive*.

The man *wrote* the letter.

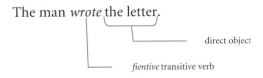

Or it may be *intransitive*.

The bees *swarm*.

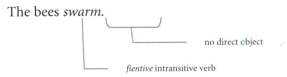

Fientive contrasts with *Stative*.

A **STATIVE** verb denotes a state, a circumstance, or quality. Most statives are intransitive.

Eglon *is heavy*.

Some, however, are transitive.

But Esau I *hate*.

Malachi 1:3

In the example above, שָׂנֵא is stative in form but clearly takes a direct object.

Stative contrasts with *Fientive*.

We can consider *fientive* and *stative* to be on a spectrum at opposite ends. The notions of *transitive* and *intransitive* are another spectrum and also at opposite ends. The following diagram may be helpful:

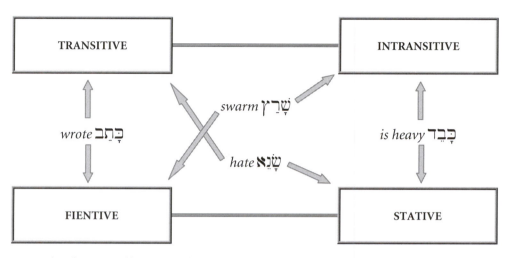

The diagram illustrates, from the examples of sentences used in this chapter, that:

wrote is fientive and transitive (*The man <u>wrote</u> the letter.*)

is heavy is stative and intransitive (*Eglon <u>is heavy</u>.*)

hate is stative and can be transitive (as used in Malachi 1:3, *Esau I <u>hate</u>.*)

swarm is fientive and usually intransitive (*The bees <u>swarm</u>.*)

TENSE

TENSE denotes when the process of a verb takes place. We can talk about **ABSOLUTE** and **RELATIVE** tense.

ENGLISH

ABSOLUTE TENSE

Absolute tense relates the **TIME** of a situation from the **PRESENT**. English has three *major* absolute tenses: **PAST**, **PRESENT**, and **FUTURE**. Each of these has sub-categories, which we shall explore. The illustration below can help us to conceptualize the absolute tenses. Each circle represents a situation and the dashed vertical line represents the moment of speaking or writing.

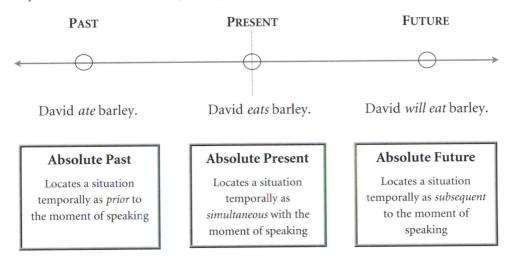

Absolute Past	**Absolute Present**	**Absolute Future**
Locates a situation temporally as *prior* to the moment of speaking	Locates a situation temporally as *simultaneous* with the moment of speaking	Locates a situation temporally as *subsequent* to the moment of speaking

Figure vi: English Absolute Tense

To each of these the notion of **PROGRESSION** can be added: a situation, relative to the moment of speaking, is viewed as being *in progress*. Progression often conveys the notion of aspect within English (see **ASPECT**, p. 92).

➤ Absolute Past Progressive: David *was eating* barley.

➤ Absolute Present Progressive: David *is eating* barley.

> Absolute Future Progressive: David *will be eating* barley.

RELATIVE TENSE

Relative tense relates the TIME of a situation to the TIME OF ANOTHER SITUATION. Conceptualize the situation of *walking down the road.*

> Relative Present Tense: When walking down the road, I *meet* Ezra.

> Relative Past Tense: When walking down the road, I *met* Ezra.

> Relative Future Tense: When walking down the road, I *will meet* Ezra.

PERFECT "TENSE"

Commonly called a *tense,* the perfect is closer to aspect because the perfect "tense" presents a view of a **state** that is the result of a **preceding situation**. Here is a way to conceptualize it.

SITUATION

STATE

Figure vii: The Perfect

Stated a bit more precisely, the perfect expresses (1) a state resulting from a prior situation and (2) the time of the prior situation. This sets the stage for different types of *perfects.*

➤ Present Perfect: David *has eaten.*

The present perfect expresses a **PRESENT** abiding **STATE** from a **PRIOR SITUATION**. The situation of *eating* has been accomplished in the past, while the state of having eaten continues to the moment of speaking.

➤ Past Perfect/Pluperfect: David *had eaten.*

The past perfect expresses a **PAST** abiding **STATE** relating to a **PRIOR SITUATION**. The situation of *eating* has been accomplished in the past, and the state of having eaten continued for a time prior to the moment of speaking.

➤ Future Perfect: David *will have eaten.*

The future perfect expresses a **FUTURE** abiding **STATE** relating to a **PRIOR SITUATION**. The situation of *eating* will be accomplished in the future, and the state of having eaten will continue for a time subsequent to the moment of speaking.

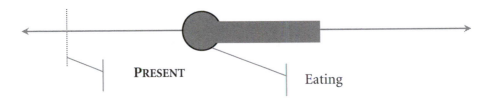

To each of these the notion of **PROGRESSION** can be added: a situation, relative to the moment of speaking, is viewed as being *in progress*.

➢ Present Perfect Progressive: David *has been eating.*

➢ Past Perfect/Pluperfect Progressive: David *had been eating.*

➢ Future Perfect Progressive: David *will have been eating.*

BIBLICAL HEBREW

I strongly suggest, before reading further, that you go directly to the English section of the chapter on **ASPECT** (p. 92). Read it, then return to this section.

Linguists of Biblical Hebrew continue to debate whether the language is primarily oriented around tense or around aspect. We shall go forward suggesting that the Suffix (Perfect) and Prefix (Imperfect) Conjugations denote primarily ASPECT.

One particular verbal form in Biblical Hebrew, however, the *vav*-consecutive plus Prefix (Imperfect) Conjugation, called the *vayyiqtol*, appears commonly to convey PAST TENSE.[6] This form is most often found in past-time narrative.

We must not think that we are forced, in any given language, into a firm *either/or* decision about tense and aspect. A particular language does not have to convey tense *to the exclusion of* aspect, or aspect *to the exclusion of* tense. Consider English. We do not have a particular form (that is, morph) that expresses aspect and that attaches itself to a verb (like some languages). In the English section of this chapter, however, you have read how the notion of *progression* in English conveys a notion of aspect.

David *ate* barley. = absolute past tense

David *was eating* barley. = absolute past progressive "tense" = aspect

---

[6] This is the recent argument of an article by John A. Cook, "The Hebrew Verb: A Grammaticalization Approach" (in preparation for publication). The article is based on the work of his dissertation, "The Biblical Hebrew Verbal System: A Grammaticalization Approach" (Ph.D. diss., Department of Hebrew and Semitic Studies, University of Wisconsin–Madison, 2002). I thank him for sharing his work with me.

The first example is seen clearly by English speakers as TENSE. The second example, however, though referred to as "tense" by many English grammars, is actually closer to conveying ASPECT.

So, we go forward suggesting that while the Suffix (Perfect) and Prefix (Imperfect) Conjugations primarily denote ASPECT, the *vav*-consecutive plus Prefix (Imperfect) Conjugation, the *vayyiqtol,* appears commonly to convey PAST TENSE.

וַיִּשְׁלַח דָּוִד אֶת־יָדוֹ אֶל־הַכֶּלִי

and-he-sent David DO-hand-his to the-bag

וַיִּקַּח מִשָּׁם אֶבֶן

then-he-took from-there stone

וַיְקַלַּע

then-he-slung

וַיַּךְ אֶת־הַפְּלִשְׁתִּי אֶל־מִצְחוֹ

then-he-struck DO-the-Philistine to brow-his

David *put* his hand into the shepherd's bag and *took* out a stone. He *hurled* it with a sling and *struck* the Philistine on his brow. 1 Samuel 17:49

ASPECT

ASPECT is a concept not very familiar to English speakers. Ironically, though, the language has numerous constructions that convey it. Aspect likely plays a role in the Suffix (Perfect) and Prefix (Imperfect) Conjugations of Biblical Hebrew. We thus need to try to understand it. You should also read the chapter on TENSE (p. 87). Reading the two chapters together should help in distinguishing the two concepts.

Aspect is the view on the *internal constituency or structure of a situation* (most any circumstance you can envision can be thought of as a situation). The categories of aspect I discuss here are the PERFECTIVE and IMPERFECTIVE (there are other categories).

English does not have a special form of the verb to disambiguate tense from aspect. Some languages, like Russian, do have special forms. Many linguists who study Biblical Hebrew consider the Suffix (Perfect) and Prefix (Imperfect) Conjugations as encoding the perfective and imperfective aspects, respectively. In English we need to try to understand aspect by exploring the meaning our many different so-called "tenses" are trying to convey.

ENGLISH

PERFECTIVE ASPECT (PERFECTIVITY)

The perfective aspect, or perfectivity, views *a situation from the outside, as whole and complete.* Be sure not to confuse this with the term PERFECT "TENSE," which I treat under the chapter TENSE, p. 87. Think of the situation of Mivtachyah having read a scroll yesterday and conceptualize it as a sphere.

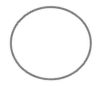

Situation: The reading of the scroll by Mivtachyah yesterday

Express the situation in English as the sentence *Mivtachyah read the scroll yesterday*. The sentence, when viewed from the standpoint of **PERFECTIVE ASPECT**, expresses the *totality* of the situation, with*out* dividing up its internal temporal structure. The *whole* situation is presented as an undivided whole. The beginning, middle, and end are rolled up into one. To help understand this, think of the many things Mivtachyah could have done yesterday in between reading the scroll: walking to and from her business, eating lunch, etc. The perfective aspect is not concerned with any of that—it makes no attempt to divide the situation into various phases.

Now think of the situation of Mivtachyah reading the scroll tomorrow. Again, think of that situation as a sphere.

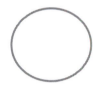

Situation: The reading of the scroll by Mivtachyah tomorrow

The English expression, *Mivtachyah will read the scroll tomorrow*, when viewed from the standpoint of **PERFECTIVE ASPECT**, still expresses the *totality* of the situation, with*out* dividing up its internal temporal structure, even though the situation has not yet occurred. The *whole* situation is still presented as an undivided whole.

English speakers, when we read such sentences, most likely see them from a standpoint of **TENSE**. Indeed, they can be viewed from the perspective of tense: one situation is oriented temporally prior to the present, the other, temporally anterior (read the chapter on **TENSE**, p. 87). Aspect, however, is *another* way to view a situation, and the perfective aspect sees a situation as whole without considering how it relates in time to the present.

Here are some more examples of what perfectivity entails.

➢ single or momentary situations

I *repaired* the wall.

He *will write* the message on the ostracon and *send* it to Azeqah.

➢ situations that have a goal of completion

Did you *finish repairing* the wall?

Will she *memorize* the paradigm?

What *did* you *do* yesterday? (what was *accomplished?*)
    — I *sacrificed* a ram. (*whole* situation)
    — And I *worked* in the garden. (*whole* situation)

What *will* you *do* tomorrow? (what will be *accomplished?*)
    — I *shall sacrifice* a ram. (*whole* situation)
    — And I *shall work* in the garden. (*whole* situation)

Again, English speakers will automatically see these sentences expressing past and future tense. From the view of perfectivity, however, they are situations viewed as a whole.

IMPERFECTIVE ASPECT (IMPERFECTIVITY)

The imperfective aspect, or imperfectivity, views *a situation from the <u>inside</u>. It considers the internal temporal structure of a situation.* Think again of our situation of Mivtachyah reading the scroll.

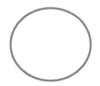

Situation: The reading of the scroll by Mivtachyah

Consider the following sentences linked to our situation:

1. Mivtachyah read the scroll yesterday.

2. While she was reading it, one of her tenants arrived.

In English, again, we can view the sentences either from a perspective of tense or aspect. From an **ASPECTUAL** perspective, sentence 1 is perfective, the situation is viewed from the outside and is whole, complete. Sentence 2, however, opens up the situation and says that some time during the situation of Mivtachyah reading her scroll, one of her tenants arrived. From a perspective of **TENSE**, sentence 1 is absolute past tense. The first (and subordinate) clause in sentence 2 is absolute past progressive, while the second (and main clause) is relative past.

Here are some more examples of what imperfectivity entails.

➢ repeated or habitual situations

I *studied* Biblical Hebrew every day.

He *will* never *repair* the wall.

She *would bake* the flat bread every morning.

➢ situations in progress (thus not complete)

They *were working* when he entered.

They *will be working* when he enters.

➢ completed situations without a view to result

What *did* you *do* yesterday? (what *activity* took place?)
    — I *sacrificed* a ram. (view on *activity*)
    — And *I worked* in the garden. (view on *activity*)

Compare this last example with the next to last one in the perfective aspect section. The sentences are identical. They can be viewed quite differently, however, from an aspectual perspective.

BIBLICAL HEBREW

Linguists of Biblical Hebrew debate whether the Suffix (Perfect) and Prefix (Imperfect) Conjugations denote primarily aspect or tense. We shall go forward suggesting that an aspectual system is more likely. Because English is not formally an aspectual language, though, our translations of Biblical Hebrew use a variety of what English speakers commonly label "tenses."

SUFFIX (PERFECT) CONJUGATION

The Suffix (Perfect) Conjugation denotes the PERFECTIVE ASPECT.

וְלַחֹ֫שֶׁךְ קָרָא לָ֫יְלָה   The darkness he *called* "Night."

night   he-*called*   and-the-darkness

Genesis 1:5

לֹא־יָדַע יַעֲקֹב כִּי רָחֵל גְּנָבָתַם   Jacob did not know that

she-*had-stolen*-them Rachel that Jacob he-knew not   Rachel *had stolen* them.

Genesis 31:32

וַיֹּ֫אמֶר מֶה עָשִׂ֫יתָ   He said, "What *have* you *done?*"

you-*have-done* what and-he-said

Genesis 4:10

אֱלֹהִים זְנַחְתָּ֫נוּ   God, you *have rejected* us.

you-*have-rejected*-us   God

Psalm 60:3

הִגַּ֫דְתִּי הַיּוֹם   I *declare* today . . .

the-day   I-*declare*

Deuteronomy 26:3

וּלְיִשְׁמָעֵאל שְׁמַעְתִּיךָ הִנֵּה בֵּרַ֫כְתִּי אֹתוֹ   Now about Ishmael:

DO-him I-*shall-bless* behold I-heard-you and-to-Ishmael   I have heard you.

I *shall bless* him.

Genesis 17:20

Here you can notice the variety of tenses we use in English to convey the perfective aspect of the Suffix (Perfect) Conjugation.

The Suffix (Perfect) Conjugation plus *vav*-consecutive, called the *veqatal*, expresses IMPERFECTIVE ASPECT, seemingly conveying the equivalent of the Prefix (Imperfect) Conjugation's ability to convey imperfectivity. 1 Samuel 1:3a–5a, cited on p. 169, demonstrates this use of the *veqatal*. The clauses labeled 3a and 4c have a *veqatal*. See especially, though, the two clauses 4c–5a. The clause 4c has a *veqatal*, while the next clause, 5a, has a Prefix (Imperfect) Conjugation verbal form. Both clauses convey the same imperfective aspectual view.

You should not, however, always link the *veqatal* with imperfectivity. It commonly expresses mood/modality (see the chapter on **MOOD**, p. 105, as well as those on **IMPERATIVE/2D PERSON VOLITION**, p. 99, **COHORTATIVE/1ST PERSON VOLITION**, p. 101, and **JUSSIVE/3D PERSON VOLITION**, p. 103).

וְאִם־ לֹא יַעַבְרוּ	חֲלוּצִים	אִתְּכֶם
with-you battle-prepared they-will-cross-over not and-if		

וְנֹאחֲזוּ	בְתֹכְכֶם	בְּאֶרֶץ	כְּנָעַן
Canaan in-land-of in-midst-your and-they-*must-be-settled*			

But if they will not cross over with you armed, they *must settle* with you in Canaan. Numbers 32:30

The first clause sets out a condition. The *veqatal*, which starts the second clause, expresses modality relative to the condition: if . . . (then) they *must settle*.

In the following example, a Prefix (Imperfect) Conjugation verb form occurs in the first clause, תַעֲבֹד. It conveys mood: Six days you *shall work*. The *veqatal*, which begins the second clause, continues to express the mood: and you *shall do* all your work.

שֵׁשֶׁת יָמִים תַּעֲבֹד
you-shall-work days six

וְעָשִׂיתָ	כָּל־מְלַאכְתֶּךָ
work-your all and-you-*shall-do*	

Six days you shall work and *(shall) do* all your work. Exodus 20:9

PREFIX (IMPERFECT) CONJUGATION

The Prefix (Imperfect) Conjugation conveys the IMPERFECTIVE ASPECT *and a great deal more*. Languages change. English has changed significantly since Beowulf, as did Biblical Hebrew before it took the form by which we know it on the pages of the Hebrew Bible. Quite a few verbal forms that at one time were unambiguous in form merged together to become what we call the Prefix (Imperfect) Conjugation. This is not the place to explore the details of how the forms all merged together.[7] I shall, instead, focus on the imperfective aspect of the Prefix (Imperfect) Conjugation.

תִּשְׁתֶּה	וּמִכֹּסוֹ	From his cup she *would drink.*
she-*would-drink*	and-from-cup-his	2 Samuel 12:3

בְשָׁנָה	שָׁנָה	יַעֲשֶׂה	וְכֵן	This he *would do* year after year.
in-year	year	he-*would-do*	and-thus	1 Samuel 1:7

תִּבְכֶּה	וּבָכֹה	עַל־יהוה	וַתִּתְפַּלֵּל	She prayed to Yahweh and *began weeping* excessively.
she-*cries*	and-crying	YHWH	to	and-she-prayed	1 Samuel 1:10

כְּגִבּוֹר	עָלַי	יָרֻץ	He *rushes* at me like a warrior.
like-warrior	at-me	he-*runs*	Job 16:14

When a Prefix (Imperfect) Conjugation form is prefixed with a *vav*-consecutive, the *vayyiqtol,* it commonly conveys PAST TENSE. See that discussion under the chapter on **TENSE**, beginning with p. 90.

---

[7] My work, *Biblical Hebrew Foundations: A Concise Historical Grammar of the Phoneme through Word* (in preparation for publication), discusses the historical mergings.

IMPERATIVE/2d PERSON VOLITION

The **IMPERATIVE** is one of the categories of the volitional mood, where the will of a speaker imposes his or her will onto an entity being addressed. You need to read the entire chapter on **MOOD** (p. 105) to understand how the imperative fits into the bigger picture of mood.

ENGLISH

The **IMPERATIVE** is a second person command. The speaker wishes to impose his or her will onto the grammatical second person. The order may be to one person or several people. The imperative commonly uses the dictionary form of the verb but no second person subject pronoun (see **PRONOUN**, p. 39), though it may occur.

> *Bow* before the king!

> *Sit* here!

> You, *stop* that!

English also expresses the imperative by *you shall + verb*. By contrast, *you will + verb* expresses the future tense (see **TENSE**, p. 87) of the indicative mood. Few English speakers keep this distinction clear.

> *You <u>shall</u> keep* the Sabbath! (= imperative)

> > The speaker is imposing his/her will onto the addressee. The addressee is expected to obey the order.

> *You <u>will</u> be* on Sinai. (= indicative mood)

> > The speaker is simply stating a fact that will occur.

BIBLICAL HEBREW

Biblical Hebrew has imperative verbal forms. These imperatives are used for positive commands. For negative second person commands, Biblical Hebrew commonly uses אַל or לֹא immediately before second person Prefix (Imperfect)

Conjugation forms. Consult your grammar book for the variety of forms for the imperative, both positive and negative.

בֹּאוּ בֵית־אֵל וּפִשְׁעוּ

and-*sin*   Bethel   *go*

Go to Bethel and *sin!*

Amos 4:4

לֹא תִּרְצָח

you-shall-murder   not

You shall not/never murder!

Exodus 20:13

אַל־תִּשְׁמְעוּ אֶל־חִזְקִיָּהוּ

Hezekiah   to   *you-shall-listen*   not

Do not listen to Hezekiah!

2 Kings 18:31

The *vav*-consecutive plus Suffix (Perfect) Conjugation, often labeled as *"veqatal,"* cast in the 2d person, also expresses 2d person volition.

אֶת־מִזְבַּח הָעֹלָה   וּמָשַׁחְתָּ

the-burnt-offering   DO-altar-of   and-*you-must-anoint*

You must anoint the burnt-offering altar.

Exodus 40:10

COHORTATIVE/1st PERSON VOLITION

FIRST PERSON VOLITION is one of the categories of the volitional mood, where the will of a speaker imposes his or her will onto an entity being addressed. The term, **COHORTATIVE**, is used commonly within Hebrew grammars to refer to first person volition. You need to read the entire chapter on **MOOD** (p. 105) to understand how the cohortative fits into the bigger picture of mood.

ENGLISH

The **FIRST PERSON VOLITION** expresses the will of the speaker alone or as part of a group. The speaker resolves to carry out a verbal process. English expresses the first person volition by *I/We will + verb*. By contrast, *I/We shall + verb* expresses the future tense (see **TENSE**, p. 87) of the indicative mood. Few English speakers keep this distinction clear.

> *I/We <u>will</u> go* to the temple. (= 1st person volition)
>> This expresses the speaker's will to go to the temple.

> *I/We <u>shall</u> go* to the temple. (= indicative mood)
>> The speaker is simply stating a fact that will occur.

Where a speaker does not have the power or authority to bring about his/her resolve, first person volition is commonly expressed by *may I/we* or *let me/us*. Be careful, the latter is spoken *by* the speaker *to* the speaker. If it were spoken to impose the speaker's will onto a second person, that would be the imperative.

> *May I/we eat* meat?
> *Let me/us pass* through.
> *Let's go* to Bethel.

BIBLICAL HEBREW

Biblical Hebrew's first person volitive is known as the **COHORTATIVE**, typically marked by הָ - on the end of the first person Prefix (Imperfect) Conjugation forms.

אֵלְכָה

I-will-go

I <u>will</u> go.

Genesis 45:28

נִכְרְתָה בְרִית

covenant   *let-us-cut*

Let us make a covenant.

Genesis 31:44

The *vav*-consecutive plus Suffix (Perfect) Conjugation, often labeled as *"veqatal,"* cast in the 1st person, also expresses 1st person volition.

אֲלַקֳטָה־נָּא וְאָסַפְתִּי

and-*let-me-gather*   let-me-glean

Let me glean and *gather.*

Ruth 2:7

JUSSIVE/3d PERSON VOLITION

THIRD PERSON VOLITION is one of the categories of the volitional mood, where the will of a speaker imposes his or her will onto an entity being addressed. The term, **JUSSIVE**, is used commonly within Hebrew grammars to refer to third person volition. You need to read the entire chapter on **MOOD** (p. 105) to understand how the jussive fits into the bigger picture of mood.

ENGLISH

The **THIRD PERSON VOLITION** is where the speaker wishes to impose his or her will onto the grammatical third person, singular or plural.

> *May YHWH bless* you.
>
> *Let him pass* through.
>
> *Long live the king!* (= *May the king live.*)
>
> *Let him go* to Bethel.

BIBLICAL HEBREW

Third person volition is commonly known as the **JUSSIVE** in Biblical Hebrew. The language, earlier in its history, likely had a full paradigm (all persons, singular and plural) known as the jussive. The jussive's form is often identical with the third person Prefix (Imperfect) Conjugation forms, though roots that are III-*he* or II-*vav/yod* show a difference (consult the paradigms in your grammar book for root-types and Stems that show a difference).

יִבְנֶה	he will build (= Qal Prefix [Imperfect] Conjugation, non-jussive form)
יִבֶן	let him build/he must build (= Qal jussive form)
יָשׁוּב	he will return (= Qal Prefix [Imperfect] Conjugation, non-jussive form)
יָשֹׁב	let him return/he must return (= Qal jussive form)

Because the jussive *form* is often ambiguous, you need to be careful that you rely on textual environment (context) to help you pick up the jussive *sense* of will or volition.

יְבָרֶכְךָ   יהוה וְיִשְׁמְרֶךָ

and-*may-he-keep*-you   YHWH   *may-he-bless*-you

May YHWH *bless* you and *keep* you.

Numbers 6:24

The *vav*-consecutive plus Suffix (Perfect) Conjugation, often labeled as *"veqatal,"* cast in the 3d person, also expresses 3d person volition.

וְהִקְרִיב ... פַּר בֶּן בָּקָר

cattle   son-of   bull ... and-*he-must-bring*

He must bring . . . a young bull.

Leviticus 4:3

MOOD

MOOD or **MODALITY** is the attitude or disposition a speaker has toward what she or he is expressing. Mood reflects the speaker's *mood*, as it were. A speaker can *declare, command, demand, wish, prohibit*, etc.

ENGLISH

Mood is conveyed through the verbal forms. We can categorize the moods as

(1) **REAL** or (2) **IRREAL**.

We refer to the real mood more commonly as the **INDICATIVE MOOD**.

Under the irreal moods we focus our attention on many different possible situations. We shall categorize the irreal moods as the **VOLITIONAL** and the **NON-VOLITIONAL**. The former is where the speaker imposes his/her will on an addressee. The latter involves an expression of the speaker's will or attitude about a situation without imposing the will. The **SUBJUNCTIVE MOOD** fits here. English also uses a variety of *modal auxiliaries (may, can, should, must, ought*, etc.), which we shall call **"MODALS,"** to convey attitudes such as **PERMISSION** (*may*), **OBLIGATION** (*should*), **CAPABILITY** (*can*), **DELIBERATION** (*should*), etc.

We thus have

(1) Real Mood = Indicative Mood;

(2) Irreal Mood;

(a) Volitional Mood;

(b) Non-Volitional Irreal Mood;

(i) Subjunctive Mood;

(ii) "Modals";

a) Permission;

b) Obligation;

c) Capability;

d) Deliberation.

REAL MOOD = INDICATIVE MOOD

Also known as the DECLARATIVE mood, because it *declares,* the real or indicative mood

➢ states a fact;

> Abraham *lived* in Hebron.
>
> Joseph *is* in Egypt.
>
> David *will return* to Jerusalem.

➢ states a possibility, a situation that can be fact.

> If Joseph *is* in Egypt, you can meet him.
>> The possibility is real that Joseph is in Egypt and you, therefore, can meet him.

The indicative conveys a verbal process that actually occurred, is occurring, or will likely occur in the future. It is the most common of the moods.

IRREAL MOOD

Volitional Mood

The volitional mood imposes the will of the speaker onto an entity being addressed. It is irreal, however, because what the speaker desires depends on whether the addressee will accede to the speaker's will. The speaker's will is thus not factual unless the addressee performs what the speaker desires. In anticipation of looking at Biblical Hebrew, we can talk about three different types of volitional moods or *volitives:*

> **Imperative/2d Person Volition;**
> **1st Person Volition;**
> **3d Person Volition.**

Imperative/2d Person Volition

The IMPERATIVE is a second person command. The speaker wishes to impose his or her will onto the grammatical second person. The order may be to one person or several people. The imperative commonly uses the dictionary form of the verb

but no second person subject pronoun (see **PRONOUN**, p. 39), though it may occur.

> *Bow* before the king!

> *Sit* here!

> You, *stop* that!

English also expresses the imperative by *you shall* + *verb*. By contrast, *you will* +
verb expresses the future tense (see **TENSE**, p. 87) of the indicative mood. Few
English speakers keep this distinction clear.

> *You shall keep* the Sabbath! (= imperative)
>> The speaker is imposing his/her will onto the addressee. The addressee is expected to obey
>> the order.

> *You will be* on Sinai. (= indicative mood)
>> The speaker is simply stating a fact that will occur.

1st Person Volition

The **FIRST PERSON VOLITION** expresses the will of the speaker alone or as part of a
group. The speaker resolves to carry out a verbal process. English expresses the
first person volition by *I/We will* + *verb*. By contrast, *I/We shall* + *verb* expresses
the future tense (see **TENSE**, p. 87) of the indicative mood. Few English speakers
keep this distinction clear.

> *I/We will go* to the temple. (= 1st person volition)
>> This expresses the speaker's will to go to the temple.

> *I/We shall go* to the temple. (= indicative mood)
>> The speaker is simply stating a fact that will occur.

Where a speaker does not have the power or authority to bring about his/her
resolve, first person volition is commonly expressed by *may I/we* or *let me/us*. Be
careful, the latter is spoken *by* the speaker *to* the speaker. If it were spoken to impose the speaker's will onto a second person, that would be the imperative.

May I/we eat meat?

Let me/us pass through.

Let's go to Bethel.

3d Person Volition

The **THIRD PERSON VOLITION** is where the speaker wishes to impose his or her will onto the grammatical third person, singular or plural.

May YHWH bless you.

Let him pass through.

Long live the king! (= *May the king live.*)

Let him go to Bethel.

Non-Volitional Irreal Mood

The non-volitional irreal mood involves an expression of the speaker's will or attitude about a situation without imposing the will.

Subjunctive Mood

The subjunctive mood commonly expresses a situation or condition that is not actual fact. Those of you who have had languages like Latin or German have had to learn paradigms of verbal forms known as the subjunctive. In English, the situation is far less complex, which accounts for a great deal of confusion for many English speakers in identifying the use of the subjunctive mood. English speakers, in fact, seem to be using it less and less. The term *subjunctive* appears to come from the fact that this mood is commonly found in subordinate clauses, that is, clauses that are *sub-joined* (see **DEPENDENT/SUBORDINATE**, p. 124, under **CLAUSE**). It can occur, however, in independent clauses.

➤ Clauses that begin with *if* and are *contrary to fact* often are in the subjunctive mood.

If I *were* you, I would run. (= subjunctive mood)

                            subordinate clause
                            verb is subjunctive mood

The verb follows *if* and expresses a non-factual or irreal condition: it is impossible for the speaker to be the other person.

If I *was* you, I would run. (= incorrect grammar)

If only we *knew* Biblical Hebrew fluently.

                                         independent clause
                                         verb is subjunctive mood

The verb follows *if* and expresses a non-factual or irreal condition: the speaker does not know Hebrew fluently

➢ Clauses that begin with *though* (= concessive, that is, conceding or acknowledging something) are often in the subjunctive mood.

Though he *be* correct, he mustn't offend her.

                              subordinate clause
                              verb is subjunctive mood

➢ Clauses that *follow* a verb that expresses a wish, a demand, a doubt, a request, or a proposal are in the subjunctive mood. Here are some verbs that often govern clauses where we use (or should use) the subjunctive: *wish, demand, request, command, suggest, prefer, ask, insist,* etc.

I *wish* (that) Elijah *were* here.

                            subordinate clause
                            verb is subjunctive mood

Pharaoh *demanded* (that) Moses *come.*

                                      subordinate clause
                                      verb is subjunctive mood

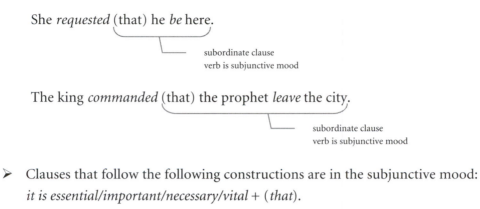

She *requested* (that) he *be* here.

                                        subordinate clause
verb is subjunctive mood

The king *commanded* (that) the prophet *leave* the city.

          subordinate clause
verb is subjunctive mood

➤ Clauses that follow the following constructions are in the subjunctive mood: *it is essential/important/necessary/vital + (that).*

It is essential (that) you *be* the leader.

          subordinate clause
verb is subjunctive mood

It was vital (that) Abigail *speak* to David.

          subordinate clause
verb is subjunctive mood

The form of the subjunctive is quite simple. The subjunctive does not change in form regardless of person (1st, 2d, 3d). With only one exception, the subjunctive form of *all* verbs is the dictionary form (= English infinitive without *to*). The one exception is *be.*

FORM OF THE SUBJUNCTIVE		
(TO) BE		OTHER VERBS: SAME AS INFINITIVE (TO) LIVE
PAST	PRESENT	PAST AND PRESENT
I *were*	I *be*	I *live*
you *were*	you *be*	you *live*
he, she, it *were*	he, she, it *be*	he, she, it *live*
we *were*	we *be*	we *live*
you *were*	you *be*	you *live*
they *were*	they *be*	they *live*

"Modals"

English also uses a variety of *modal auxiliaries* (*may, can, should, must, ought,* etc.), which we have called "modals."

➢ Permission: conveys the speaker's permission for the addressee to carry out a verbal process.

You *may feed* the children.

You *may live* on my holy hill.

➢ Obligation: conveys what the speaker or addressee considers necessary, an obligation.

You *should go* to Jerusalem.

This is what I *should do*.

➢ Capability: conveys the speaker or addressee's capability to perform a verbal process.

You *can leave* the prison now, Joseph.

A stone *could kill* Goliath.

➢ Deliberation: conveys the speaker or addressee's deliberation on whether to carry out a verbal process. This is commonly found in question form.

Should we *attend* the feast in Jerusalem?

Should you *live* by the river?

BIBLICAL HEBREW

Mood is conveyed through the verbal forms. We can categorize the moods as

(1) REAL or (2) IRREAL.

We refer to the real mood more commonly as the INDICATIVE MOOD.

We shall categorize the irreal moods, as we did for English, as the VOLITIONAL and the NON-VOLITIONAL. We do not, however, formally talk of the subjunctive mood in Biblical Hebrew. Hebrew likely made use of the subjunctive at an earlier stage of the language—Arabic (a related Semitic language) has a special subjunctive verb form. The meaning of the subjunctive lives on but is not conveyed in a special form of the verb. Hebrew grammars do not treat the subjunctive and neither shall I. We can talk, though, of irreal "modals" such as PERMISSION, OBLIGATION, CAPABILITY, DELIBERATION, etc.

We thus have

       (1) Real Mood = Indicative Mood;

       (2) Irreal Mood;

          (a) Volitional Mood;

          (b) Non-Volitional Irreal Mood;

             (i) Permission;

             (ii) Obligation;

             (iii) Capability;

             (iv) Deliberation.

REAL MOOD = INDICATIVE MOOD

The Suffix (Perfect) and Prefix (Imperfect) Conjugations commonly convey the indicative mood.

Suffix (Perfect) Conjugation

מָלַךְ דָּוִד עַל־יִשְׂרָאֵל

Israel over David *reigned*

David *reigned* over Jerusalem.

1 Kings 2:11

Prefix (Imperfect) Conjugation

הַשֹּׁחַד יְעַוֵּר פִּקְחִים

officials *blinds* the-bribe

The bribe *blinds* officials.

Exodus 23:8

IRREAL MOOD

Volitional Mood

Biblical Hebrew has three different types of volitional moods or *volitives*, each with distinctive verbal forms.

Imperative/2d Person Volition
Cohortative/1st Person Volition
Jussive/3d Person Volition

Imperative/2d Person Volition

Biblical Hebrew has imperative verbal forms. These imperatives are used for positive commands. For negative second person commands, Biblical Hebrew commonly uses אַל or לֹא immediately before second person Prefix (Imperfect) Conjugation forms. Consult your grammar book for the variety of forms for the imperative, both positive and negative.

בֹּאוּ בֵית־אֵל וּפִשְׁעוּ		*Go* to Bethel and *sin!*
and-*sin* Bethel *go*		Amos 4:4

לֹא תִּרְצָח	*You shall not/never murder!*
you-shall-murder not	Exodus 20:13

אֶל־הִזְקִיָּהוּ אַל־תִּשְׁמְעוּ		*Do not listen* to Hezekiah!
Hezekiah to you-shall-listen not		2 Kings 18:31

The *vav*-consecutive plus Suffix (Perfect) Conjugation, often labeled as *"veqatal,"* cast in the 2d person, also expresses 2d person volition.

אֶת־מִזְבַּח הָעֹלָה וּמָשַׁחְתָּ		*You must anoint* the burnt-offering altar.
the-burnt-offering DO-altar-of and-*you-must-anoint*		Exodus 40:10

Cohortative/1st Person Volition

Biblical Hebrew's first person volitive is known as the **COHORTATIVE**, typically marked by הָ - on the end of the first person Prefix (Imperfect) Conjugation forms.

אֵלְכָה	*I will go.*
I-will-go	Genesis 45:28

נִכְרְתָה בְרִית

covenant *let-us-cut*

Let us make a covenant.

Genesis 31:44

The *vav*-consecutive plus Suffix (Perfect) Conjugation, often labeled as *"veqatal,"* cast in the 1st person, also expresses 1st person volition.

אֶלְקֳטָה־נָּא וְאָסַפְתִּי

and-*let-me-gather*   *let-me-glean*

Let me glean and *gather.*

Ruth 2:7

Jussive/3d Person Volition

Third person volition is commonly known as the JUSSIVE in Biblical Hebrew. The language, earlier in its history, likely had a full paradigm (all persons, singular and plural) known as the jussive. The jussive's form is often identical with the third person Prefix (Imperfect) Conjugation forms, though roots that are III-*he* or II-*vav/yod* show a difference (consult the paradigms in your grammar book for root-types and Stems that show a difference).

יִבְנֶה he will build (= Qal Prefix [Imperfect] Conjugation, non-jussive form)

יִבֶן let him build/he must build (= Qal jussive form)

יָשׁוּב he will return (= Qal Prefix [Imperfect] Conjugation, non-jussive form)

יָשֹׁב let him return/he must return (= Qal jussive form)

Because the jussive *form* is often ambiguous, you need to be careful that you rely on textual environment (context) to help you pick up the jussive *sense* of will or volition.

May YHWH bless you and *keep* you.

and-*may-he-keep-you* YHWH *may-he-bless-you*

Numbers 6:24

The *vav*-consecutive plus Suffix (Perfect) Conjugation, often labeled as *"veqatal,"* cast in the 3d person, also expresses 3d person volition.

וְהִקְרִיב ... פַּר בֶּן־בָּקָר

cattle son-of bull . . . and-*he-must-bring*

He must bring . . . a young bull.

Leviticus 4:3

Non-Volitional Irreal Mood

The Prefix (Imperfect) Conjugation commonly conveys other irreal moods that Hebrew grammarians simply call "modals."

➤ Permission: conveys the speaker's permission for the addressee to carry out a verbal process.

אֶת־שְׁנֵי בָנַי תָּמִית

you-may-kill sons-my DO-two-of

My two sons *you may kill.*

Genesis 42:37

➤ Obligation: conveys what the speaker or addressee considers necessary, an obligation.

וְהוֹרֵיתִי אֶתְכֶם אֵת אֲשֶׁר תַּעֲשׂוּן

you-should-do what DO DO-you and-I-shall-teach

I shall teach you what *you should do.*

Exodus 4:15

➤ Capability: conveys the speaker or addressee's capability to perform a verbal process.

וְחָרָשׁ לֹא יִמָּצֵא

he-can-be-found not and-a-metalworker

A metal worker *could* not *be found.*

1 Samuel 13:19

➤ Deliberation: conveys the speaker or addressee's deliberation on whether to carry out a verbal process. This is commonly found in question form.

הַכְזוֹנָה יַעֲשֶׂה אֶת־אֲחוֹתֵנוּ

DO-sister-our he-should-treat INTERROG-like-a-prostitute

Should he *have treated* our sister like a prostitute?

Genesis 34:31

VOICE

VOICE refers either to (1) a fundamental part in producing sound (see SOUND PRODUCTION, p. 7) or (2) a relationship between the grammatical subject, the verb, and adverbials. This chapter focuses solely on the latter.

We need to understand the *syntactic* notions of SUBJECT (see SUBJECT, p. 126) and DIRECT OBJECT (see DIRECT/OBJECTIVE ACCUSATIVE, p. 135, under PREDICATE/PREDICATION) and the semantic roles of AGENT and PATIENT (see SEMANTICS: PROCESSES, ROLES, AND CIRCUMSTANCES, p. 143). For the purpose of our discussion here, I want to define the semantic roles of *agent* and *patient* more broadly than I do in the chapter on SEMANTICS: PROCESSES, ROLES, AND CIRCUMSTANCES.

- agent: the semantic concept referring to an entity responsible for a process

- patient: the semantic concept referring to the entity receiving a process

In a clause, we may find a word or word-grouping that is the grammatical *subject* as well as the semantic *agent.* The *subject* and *agent* labels refer to that same word or word-grouping from two different perspectives. One is from the perspective of *syntax,* the other from *semantic roles.* Sometimes we find a word or word-grouping that is the grammatical *direct object* as well as the semantic *patient.*

Subject, direct object, agent, and patient are important in understanding voice. With English and Biblical Hebrew in mind, we can talk about four voices: (1) active, (2) passive, (3) middle, and (4) reflexive.

ENGLISH

ACTIVE VOICE

The active voice is expressed when the grammatical subject is also the semantic agent. The subject performs the verb's process. Look at an example where the verb is *intransitive* (does not govern a direct object).

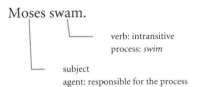

Moses swam.

verb: intransitive
process: *swim*

subject
agent: responsible for the process

Now consider an example where the verb is *transitive* (governs a direct object).

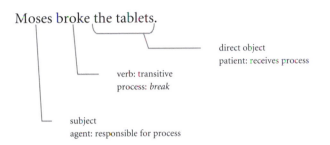

Moses broke the tablets.

direct object
patient: receives process

verb: transitive
process: *break*

subject
agent: responsible for process

When the verb is transitive and we thus have a direct object, the direct object is also the semantic patient.

➤ The active voice then is expressed when:

the subject is the agent (and the direct object is the patient).

PASSIVE VOICE

The passive voice is expressed when the grammatical subject is also the semantic patient. The subject receives the verb's process. Further, an agent is in mind, whether explicitly expressed or not.

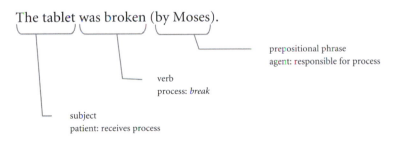

The tablet was broken (by Moses).

prepositional phrase
agent: responsible for process

verb
process: *break*

subject
patient: receives process

➤ The passive voice then is expressed when:

the subject is the patient and an agent is in mind, whether explicit or implicit.

MIDDLE VOICE

The middle voice is expressed when the grammatical subject is also the semantic patient **but no agent is in mind**.

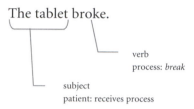

The tablet broke.

verb
process: *break*

subject
patient: receives process

The lack of a semantic agent is very important in the definition. You may notice that a person may try to use the middle voice to describe a verbal process in a way to "hide" agency. For example, if someone were responsible for breaking a window, that person might use the middle voice, *The window broke!*, instead of *I broke the window!* (active voice). The middle voice diminishes agency. Not all verbs can be expressed in the middle voice.

➤   The middle voice then is expressed when:

the subject is the patient and no agent is in mind.

REFLEXIVE VOICE

The reflexive voice is expressed when the grammatical subject is the semantic agent and patient. The subject both performs and receives the verb's process. In English, a reflexive pronoun (a pronoun that refers back to the subject) functions as a direct object.

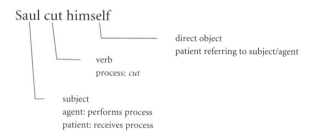

Saul cut himself

direct object
patient referring to subject/agent

verb
process: *cut*

subject
agent: performs process
patient: receives process

118

> ➤ The reflexive voice then is expressed when:

the subject is the semantic agent and patient and a reflexive pronoun stands as a direct object and refers to the subject.

BIBLICAL HEBREW

Biblical Hebrew conveys the same four voices primarily through its system of Stems.

ACTIVE VOICE

Hebrew conveys the active voice primarily through the:

➤ Qal Stem, except for its passive participle;

➤ Piel Stem;

➤ Hifil Stem.

PASSIVE VOICE

Hebrew conveys the passive voice primarily through the:

➤ Nifal Stem;

➤ Pual Stem;

➤ Hofal Stem.

MIDDLE VOICE

Hebrew conveys the middle voice primarily through the:

➤ Nifal Stem.

REFLEXIVE VOICE

Hebrew conveys the reflexive voice primarily through the:

➤ Nifal Stem;

➤ Hitpael Stem.

We need to understand that syntactically Biblical Hebrew forms the reflexive quite differently from English. Hebrew does not use a reflexive pronoun in the direct object slot. Consider English again:

He guarded himself.

He is the word (pronoun) that functions as subject and agent, *himself* is the word (reflexive pronoun) that functions as direct object and patient. Here the Subject is also the Patient.

Now consider how Biblical Hebrew can convey this expression. It can use the Nifal Stem.

נִשְׁמַר   He guarded himself.

The Nifal verb is inflected to represent the subject and agent (3ms). But notice that no separate word (reflexive pronoun) represents the direct object or patient. The patient, however, exists semantically within this Nifal Suffix (Perfect) Conjugation 3ms form.

Part III

The Clause and Beyond

CLAUSE

A **CLAUSE** is a language unit referring to a string of words (a **SYNTAGM**) that involves a **SUBJECT** and a **COMMENT** about the subject. The comment is known as the **PREDICATE**. We commonly talk of two foremost types of clauses: (1) **INDEPENDENT** and **MAIN** and (2) **DEPENDENT** or **SUBORDINATE**.

INDEPENDENT AND MAIN

A clause that stands on its own, with its own complete thought is an independent clause. The terms *independent* and *main* are not completely synonymous. When an independent clause has a dependent or subordinate clause linked to it, we use *main* to refer to it. An *independent* clause has no dependent/subordinate clause linked to it.

ENGLISH

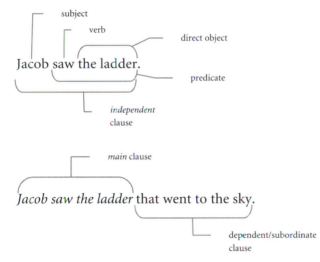

BIBLICAL HEBREW

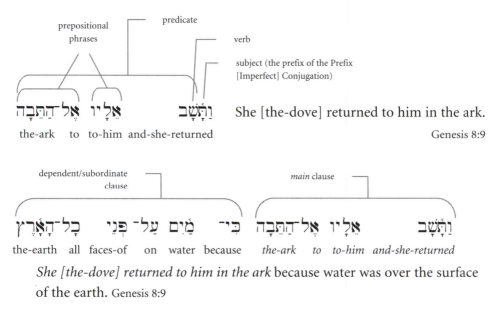

She [the-dove] returned to him in the ark.

Genesis 8:9

She [the-dove] returned to him in the ark because water was over the surface of the earth. Genesis 8:9

DEPENDENT OR SUBORDINATE

A clause that does not stand on its own and must be linked to a main clause is a dependent or subordinate clause. The terms *dependent* and *subordinate* are quite synonymous, unlike *independent* and *main*.

ENGLISH

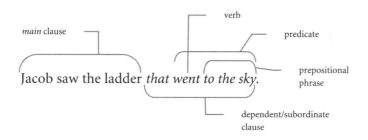

124

BIBLICAL HEBREW

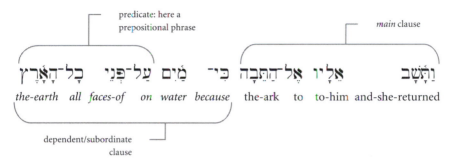

She [the-dove] returned to him in the ark *because water was over the surface of the earth.* Genesis 8:9

SUBJECT

A SUBJECT is a label for a grammatical function traditionally associated with the entity that carries out the process of a verb or about which a comment is made.

ENGLISH

To find the subject of a clause, look for a verb and ask *who?* or *what?* before saying the verb. The answer is the clause's subject.

Amos traveled to Bethel.

        subject

    Who traveled to Bethel? *Amos* = subject

The caravan arrived.

        subject

    What arrived? *The caravan* = subject

Goliath is tall.

        subject

    Who is tall? *Goliath* = subject

BIBLICAL HEBREW

As a rule the subject behaves the same way in Biblical Hebrew as it does in English. Keep in mind:

➤ The subject is already a part of the verb form in the Suffix (Perfect) and Prefix (Imperfect) Conjugations. A separate word functioning as subject is not always necessary.

➤ Hebrew has clauses that are verbless. As a *general* rule, if one word or word-grouping in such a clause is definite and one is indefinite, the subject is the definite one. See VERBLESS PREDICATION, p. 127, under PREDICATE/PREDICATION.

PREDICATE/PREDICATION

We can view a clause as having two primary components: a subject (S) and a **PREDICATE** (P). In English, the predicate has a verb and may have other words related to the verb, what we call **ADVERBIALS** (see **ADVERB**, p. 69 and the discussion below in this chapter under **VERBAL PREDICATION**).

For Biblical Hebrew every time you encounter a clause, ask this question:

> Does this clause have **VERBLESS** or **VERBAL** predication?

Verbless and verbal predication are the two options for predication in Biblical Hebrew.

VERBLESS PREDICATION

For verbless predication, Biblical Hebrew uses *no finite verbal form* (for a definition of *finite,* see under **VERB**, p. 84) in the clause. Verbless predication is expressed in two primary ways. (1) Most commonly nominals (see **NOMINAL**, p. 36) simply sit side-by-side,[8] or (2) a participle—a non-finite word form—conveys a verbal process (see under the sub-section **PREDICATE FUNCTION**, p. 79 in the **PARTICIPLE** chapter). The former concept of nominals sitting side-by-side is odd to English speakers because English commonly uses *linking verbs.*

(English does, however, have a construction similar to this Hebrew one. Think of knocking on a door with the intent of finding whether anybody is present on the other side of the door. "You there?" is a verbless clause variant of "You are there?/Are you there?" which uses a linking verb, *are.*)

The order of S(ubject) and P(redicate) is important. As a general rule, but only as a very general one, S–P is the syntax of an **IDENTIFICATORY** or **EQUATIVE** clause, while P–S is the syntax of a **DESCRIPTIVE** or **ASCRIPTIVE** or **CLASSIFICATORY**

---

[8] We sometimes encounter whole clauses that function as a subject or a predicate in a verbless clause. See an example under the sub-section **INDEPENDENT RELATIVE CLAUSE**, p. 57 in the **PRONOUN** chapter.

clause. After discussing five types of verbless predication in Biblical Hebrew, I shall return to the S–P vs. P–S issue.

ADJECTIVE PREDICATE

An adjective can stand as the predicate in a verbless clause. The adjective is known as a **PREDICATE ADJECTIVE** and agrees with the subject in number and gender, but *not* in definiteness:

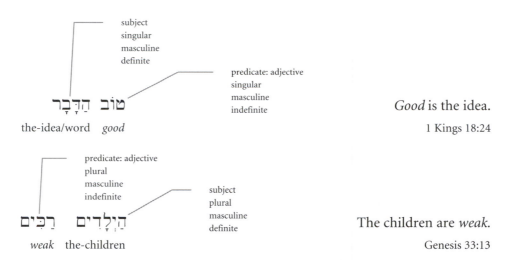

subject
singular
masculine
definite

predicate: adjective
singular
masculine
indefinite

טוֹב הַדָּבָר

the-idea/word   *good*

Good is the idea.

1 Kings 18:24

predicate: adjective
plural
masculine
indefinite

subject
plural
masculine
definite

רַכִּים   הַיְלָדִים

weak   the-children

The children are *weak*.

Genesis 33:13

For English, notice how we need to insert a linking verb in each of the examples (*is, are*). Traditionally, grammarians have suggested that the first example with its P–S syntax (predicate first) may be used to answer the question, What is the idea? *Good* is the idea (= descriptive/classificatory). The second example with its S–P syntax may be used to answer the question, Who is weak? *The children* are weak (= identificatory).

ADVERB(IAL) PREDICATE

A *prepositional phrase* or *locative adverb* (one that points to a *location*) can stand as the predicate in a verbless clause. One view of prepositions is to regard them as nominals used *ad-verbally,* though viewing the prefixed, monograph (single-consonant) prepositions (בְּ, כְּ, לְ) as true nominals seems to present a problem. Regardless of whether all prepositions are true nominals, they often have an adverbial function. Some grammarians have thus categorized prepositional phrases when used in verbless clauses as adverb(ial phrase) predicates.

➢ prepositional phrase

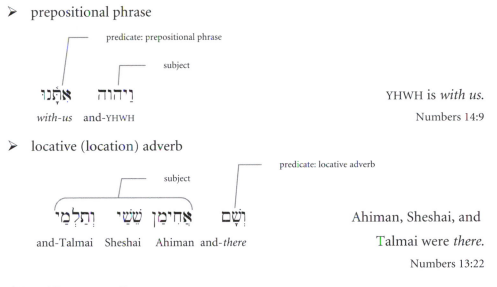

predicate: prepositional phrase

subject

אִתָּנוּ   וַיהוָה

with-us   and-YHWH

YHWH is *with us.*

Numbers 14:9

➢ locative (location) adverb

subject

predicate: locative adverb

וְתַלְמַי   שֵׁשַׁי   אֲחִימָן   וְשָׁם

and-Talmai   Sheshai   Ahiman   and-*there*

Ahiman, Sheshai, and Talmai were *there.*

Numbers 13:22

(NON-)EXISTENCE PREDICATE

To state that something exists, the common noun (or substantive) יֵשׁ *being, existence* can be used in the construct state. We say this type of clause has a predicator of existence. For non-existence, the common noun אַיִן *nothing* can be used in the construct state, אֵין. We say this type of clause has a predicator of non-existence.

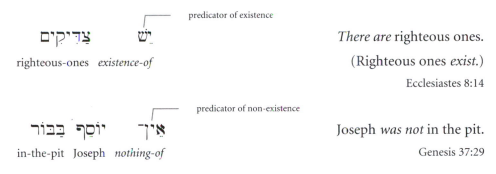

predicator of existence

צַדִּיקִים   יֵשׁ

righteous-ones   *existence-of*

There are righteous ones.

(Righteous ones *exist.*)

Ecclesiastes 8:14

predicator of non-existence

בַּבּוֹר   יוֹסֵף   אֵין־

in-the-pit   Joseph   *nothing-of*

Joseph *was not* in the pit.

Genesis 37:29

SUBSTANTIVE PREDICATE

Two nouns/substantives (or phrases involving noun/substantives) or a noun/substantive and pronoun can stand side-by-side to indicate predication. When the predicate is a noun/substantive or noun/substantival phrase, this is a *substantive predicate*. A variety of examples include:

➤ substantive juxtaposed to substantive;

The altar was wood.

Ezekiel 41:22

➤ substantive juxtaposed to proper noun;

His name was "*Jesse.*"

1 Samuel 17:12

➤ substantive juxtaposed to pronoun;

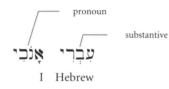

A Hebrew I am.

Jonah 1:9

➤ substantival phrase juxtaposed to pronoun.

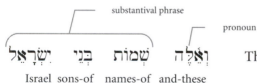

These are the names of the Israelites

Exodus 1:1

PARTICIPLE PREDICATE

A participle is commonly used as a predicator in a *verbless* clause. Though a *predicate participle* in Biblical Hebrew seems to approximate the *function* of a finite verb, a clause with a predicate participle is nevertheless considered verbless. This use of the participle does not formally convey aspect/tense and mood, which is what a finite verb, by definition, does. The finite verbal forms in the context surrounding a predicate participle inform us of where to root the participle in terms of aspect/time and mood. For examples, see **PARTICIPLE**, under **PREDICATE FUNCTION**, p. 79.

S–P vs. P–S

Returning now to the S–P vs. P–S issue, we can, for example, look at the independent, substantive predicate verbless clause. Traditionally, grammarians have made the following semantic distinctions:

➢ S–P: a structure that conveys *identification;*

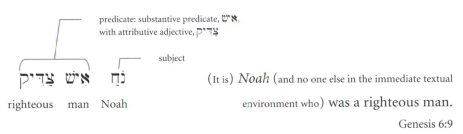

(It is) *Noah* (and no one else in the immediate textual environment who) was a righteous man.

Genesis 6:9

➢ P–S: a structure that conveys *classification* or *description.*

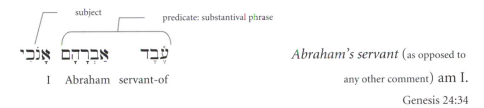

Abraham's servant (as opposed to any other comment) am I.

Genesis 24:34

This, however, is not always so simple or likely always correct. We need always to consider the wider textual environment (the **DISCOURSE**). Take the example of two conjoined verbless clauses from 1 Samuel 17:33:

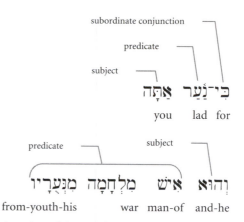

For you are a boy, but he has been a warrior since his youth. 1 Samuel 17:33

The first clause, after the conjunction כִּי, is P–S. Here, consistent with a traditional understanding, the clause conveys *classification:* What is he? A boy.

The second clause, though, does not function according to a traditional understanding in this particular textual environment. The syntax is S–P. The clause's function, however, is not *identificatory.* The clause is not conveying "(It is) HE (who) has been a warrior since his youth." Rather, the clause functions as *contrastive* classification: you're only a boy while he's a seasoned warrior. In the chapter **DISCOURSE ANALYSIS**, I discuss the concept of *markedness for focus* (p. 159), the salient and most prominent information in a clause. Suffice it to say here that the second clause is marked and conveys contrastive counter-presuppositional classification. Its S–P syntax does not convey identification.

We move on to another important consideration in verbless clauses: the use of demonstrative/personal pronouns הוּא and הִיא and their plural counterparts. Some refer to these pronouns as **PLEONASTIC** (*dummy* or *redundant*) when used in verbless predication where S and P are already filled with a word or word-group. They seemingly cloud an S–P vs. P–S distinction.

132

➤ S–pronoun–P

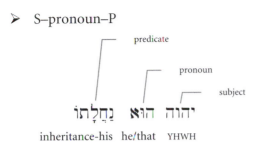

inheritance-his   he/that   YHWH

YHWH is his inheritance/heritage.

Deuteronomy 10:9

This clause expresses *identification*.

➤ S–P–pronoun

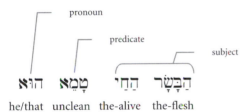

he/that   unclean   the-alive   the-flesh

The ulcer (raw flesh) is unclean.

Leviticus 13:15

This clause expresses classification/description.

The *S–pronoun–P* clause presents little trouble since a basic S–P syntax is preserved, though the pronoun is interjected between the two. The *S–P–pronoun* clause, however, which shows an apparent S–P syntax with pronoun following, is actually conveying description or classification, not identification, which S–P usually does.

We can analyze the clauses in the following way to help preserve a clearer S–P vs. P–S distinction. Waltke and O'Connor suggest that the first word or word-group be separated out as *focus,* that is, as most informationally salient or prominent (see the **MARKEDNESS FOR FOCUS AND CONNECTIVITY** section, p. 159, under **DISCOURSE ANALYSIS**)—the word or word-group that is *in focus* so to speak.[9] The remaining words or word-groups are analyzed as S or P. Let us revisit the last two clauses with this insight.

---

[9] *Introduction to Biblical Hebrew Syntax,* 130–32.

As for YHWH, he is his inheritance/heritage.

Deuteronomy 10:9

This clause, now analyzed as *Focus–S–P*, expresses *identification*.

As for the ulcer (raw flesh), unclean it is.

Leviticus 13:15

This clause, now analyzed as *Focus–P–S*, expresses *classification/description*.

VERBAL PREDICATION

In Biblical Hebrew a clause with verbal predication has a subject and a predicate. The predicate has a verb and may have **ADVERBIALS**. Dividing adverbials into two main categories is helpful: (1) **DIRECT/OBJECTIVE ACCUSATIVES** and (2) **ADVERBIAL MODIFIERS**. Here is an illustration of the concepts we shall explore.

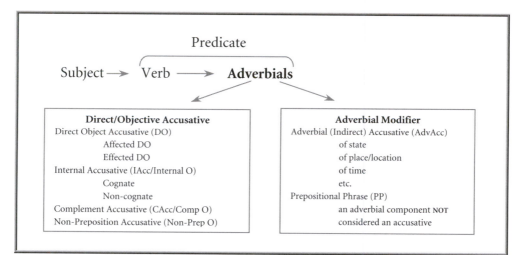

Adverb(ial)s

134

Some linguists distinguish between adverbials that are *complements* (in a sense of "*complete*-ment") and those that are *adjuncts*. The former refers to a *necessary* constituent, one needed for completeness, the latter, an *unnecessary* or *optional* one.[10] For example, in Biblical Hebrew, the direct object is a complement while an adverbial accusative is an adjunct. The distinction between what is truly a complement or an adjunct can be a fuzzy line.

Biblical Hebrew is already at a point in the history of the Hebrew language where case endings have disappeared. Hebrew once had nominative, accusative, and genitive cases, which were conveyed through morphs or forms (vowels *-u, -a, -i,* and others) that were a part of a word. We no longer have case endings to help us analyze Biblical Hebrew syntax. The relationships between the parts of a clause, however, remain, and we must be able to describe them.

DIRECT/OBJECTIVE ACCUSATIVE

Verbs can govern objects. Many verbs that govern objects are fientive in addition to being transitive (see under **VERB**, p. 84 for definitions). Such verbs can *affect* an object or *effect* one: an *affected* object is understood as one existing prior to the action ("He sowed seeds"; "He struck the rock") while an *effected* object is produced by the action itself ("He raised crops"; "He built a house"). Many verbs have objects that are virtually implied in the verb itself ("God struck a blow"), which we call "internal objects."

If one adopts the terms *complement* and *adjunct* used broadly, the direct/objective accusative is the former. Do not confuse this broader sense of *complement* (as a contrast to *adjunct*) with a more specific use to refer to the complement accusative I discuss below.

---

[10] John Lyons, *Introduction to Theoretical Linguistics* (Cambridge: Cambridge University Press, 1968), 43–50.

135

Direct Object Accusative (DO)

The direct object may be *affected*. It receives a transitive verb's process.

אֶת־הַזְּרֹעַ   הַכֹּהֵן   וְלָקַח   The priest is to take *the arm/shoulder.*
DO-the-arm   the-priest   and-he-will-take   Numbers 6:19

The direct object may also be *effected,* that is, be the result or effect of a transitive verb's process.

דֶּשֶׁא   הָאָרֶץ   תַּדְשֵׁא   Let the earth produce *grass/vegetation.*
shoots   the-earth   she-will-shoot-forth   Genesis 1:11

Many times, as the last example shows, the object has the same root as the verb. In these cases, one can talk of *cognate-effected* direct objects.

Internal Accusative (IAcc or Internal O)

The internal accusative makes a comment about the verb's action. Most internal accusatives are cognate with the verb: they share the same root. A fuzzy line separates internal accusatives, which are direct/objective accusatives, from adverbial or indirect ones. As a working rule, an internal accusative is

➤ where the accusative is making a comment on the verb's action and is based on the same root as the verb (**COGNATE INTERNAL ACCUSATIVE**), or

➤ where קוֹל *voice/sound* is used along with a verb that refers to an emission of the voice (**NON-COGNATE INTERNAL ACCUSATIVE**). Many grammarians see such objects as so much a part of the verb that they see them as *internal* or *within* or a *part* of the verb.

Cognate Internal Accusative

The adverbial makes a comment about the verb's process and is based on the same root as the verb.

פָּחַד   פָּחֲדוּ   They were overwhelmed *with dread.*
fear   they-feared   Psalm 14:5

Understand that פָּחַד is making a comment *about* the verbal process of *fearing*. פָּחַד could be a direct object *if* the writer meant to say that people were afraid of fear—they feared fear. They often were fearful, for example, and are now afraid of the fear that takes hold of them. This meaning, however, is not what the writer intends (understood from the context)—they are filled *with* fear.

Non-Cognate Internal Accusative

The word קוֹל is used with a verb that refers to the emission of voice.

קוֹל אֶחָד	כָּל־הָעָם	וַיַּעַן	All the people answered
one voice	the-people all	and-*they-answered*	*with one voice.*

Exodus 24:3

קוֹל גָּדוֹל	בְּאָזְנַי	וְקָרְאוּ	though they may cry *loudly* to me
large voice	in-ears-my	and-*they-will-call*	Ezekiel 8:18

Complement Accusative (CAcc or **Comp O**)

The complement accusative is commonly associated with *intransitive* verbs that belong to particular semantic fields, a field that has related meanings:

'abundance' (e.g., מָלֵא);

'flow' (e.g., נָזַל);

'scarcity' (e.g., חָסֵר);

'wearing/taking off clothes' (e.g., פָּשַׁט/לָבֵשׁ).

The last semantic field includes many verbs that are both intransitive and transitive.

As with internal accusatives, a fuzzy line separates complement accusatives from adverbial or indirect ones. A general rule of thumb, though, is that verbs within the semantic fields just mentioned take complement accusatives rather than adverbial accusatives. The former is somehow regarded as *necessary* with the verb while adverbial accusatives, as adjuncts, are somehow not *as* necessary. This can be a difficult distinction to make, however.

וְשָׁרַץ   הַיְאֹר   צְפַרְדְּעִים   The Nile will swarm *with frogs.*

frogs   the-Nile   and-it-will-swarm   Exodus 7:28

Again, keep in mind that the verb שָׁרַץ *swarm* is not directly affecting צְפַרְדְּעִים *frogs.* The Nile is here not swarming frogs, that is, inundating them. Frogs are thus not the direct object. The river, rather, is teeming with frogs, it is full of them. They are swarming in the Nile.

Non-Preposition Accusative (Non-Prep O)

This is also known as the so-called *datival* accusative. Admittedly a cumbersome label, the *non-preposition accusative* label has the advantage of not interjecting into Semitic languages a case that does not properly exist. The three case vowels (on singular nominals) that did at one time occur are conveniently labeled by grammarians as nominative (*/-u/), accusative (*/-a/), and genitive (*/-i/). We could, however, be less Indo-European in the labels we commonly use for a Semitic language. We could, for example, refer to the nominative as the *subject case,* the accusative as the *verb-governed case,* and the genitive as the *nominal-governed case.*

The non-preposition accusative refers to a *pronominal* object where one could expect it to be the object of a preposition. Compare:

This is **NOT** a non-preposition accusative. A preposition is present. YHWH is the object of the preposition. The verb here is governing an adverbial modifier, here a prepositional phrase. This is commonly what we see in the Hebrew Bible.

וַיִּזְעַק   שְׁמוּאֵל   אֶל־יהוה   Samuel cried *to Yahweh.*

YHWH   to   Samuel and-he-cried   1 Samuel 7:9

This **IS** a non-preposition accusative. Here ךְ- is a *pronominal* object of the verb. We expect it to be the object of a preposition, but it is not. English needs a preposition in its translation.

וַיִּזְעָקוּךְ   They cried *to you.*

and-they-cried-*you*   Nehemiah 9:28

138

ADVERBIAL MODIFIER

Two common types of adverbial modifiers are **ADVERBIAL ACCUSATIVES** and **PREPOSITIONAL PHRASES**.

Adverbial or Indirect Accusative (AdvAcc)

The adverbial or indirect accusative is

➢ *indirectly* governed by the verb, and

➢ refers to *circumstances* associated with an action or an event.

If one adopts the terms *complement* and *adjunct* used broadly, the adverbial or indirect accusative is the latter. The following categories are not exhaustive.

Adverbial Accusative of State

This specifies a state or quality of the subject or the object at the time of the verbal process or in some relation to the process. An adverbial accusative of state element is grammatically indefinite. An adverbial accusative of state is most commonly

➢ an adjective,

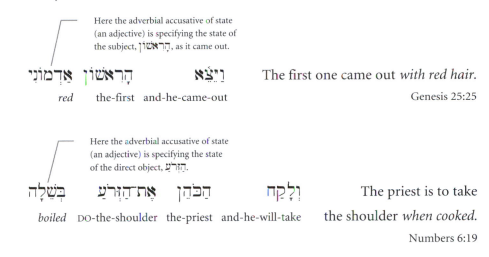

Here the adverbial accusative of state (an adjective) is specifying the state of the subject, הָרִאשׁוֹן, as it came out.

אַדְמוֹנִי	הָרִאשׁוֹן	וַיֵּצֵא
red	the-first	and-he-came-out

The first one came out *with red hair.*

Genesis 25:25

Here the adverbial accusative of state (an adjective) is specifying the state of the direct object, הַזְּרֹעַ.

בְּשֵׁלָה	אֶת־הַזְּרֹעַ	הַכֹּהֵן	וְלָקַח
boiled	DO-the-shoulder	the-priest	and-he-will-take

The priest is to take the shoulder *when cooked.*

Numbers 6:19

139

➤ a participle,

Here the adverbial accusative of
state (a participle) is specifying the
state of the direct object, הָעָם.

בֹּכֶה   אֶת־הָעָם מֹשֶׁה וַיִּשְׁמַע   Moses heard the people *crying.*

crying   DO-the-people   Moses   and-he-heard   Numbers 11:10

➤ or a substantive.

יָחַד   וַיֵּאָסְפוּ   They assembled *together.*

together   and-they-were-assembled   2 Samuel 10:15

רֹאשׁ   יְשׁוּפְךָ הוּא   He will crush you *on the head.*

head   he-will-crush-you   he   Genesis 3:15

The last example is an adverbial accusative of state and not place (*on* the head)
because the clause conveys that someone will be *fatally* crushed—crushed to the
state of death.

Adverbial Accusative of Place/Location

This specifies the location of the verb's process, usually without movement.
Commonly we see that a preposition is used in Biblical Hebrew for this, like it is
in English. When location is conveyed with the use of a preposition, the adverbial
modifier is a *prepositional phrase*. When place or location is conveyed *without* a
preposition, however, we are looking at an adverbial accusative of place.

Location is here specified without a
preposition being used in Biblical Hebrew. In
translating to English, we supply a preposition.

הָאֹהֶל   פֶּתַח־ יֹשֵׁב וְהוּא   While he was sitting *at the tent entrance.*

the-tent   *opening-of*   sitting   and-he   Genesis 18:1

הַשָּׂדֶה   וְצֵא   Go out *to the field* (with motion).

the-field   and-you-go-out!   Genesis 27:3

וַיָּשֶׂם שָׁם אֶת־הָאָדָם

DO-the-man *there* and-he-placed

He placed the man *there.*

Genesis 2:8

Adverbial Accusative of Time

This specifies the time of the verb's process or its duration.

עֶרֶב וָבֹקֶר וְצָהֳרַיִם אָשִׂיחָה

I-cry-out and-*noon* and-*morning* *evening*

Evening, morning, and *noon* I cry out in distress.

Psalm 55:18

כִּי יָמִים רַבִּים יֵשְׁבוּ בְּנֵי יִשְׂרָאֵל

Israel sons-of they-dwell *many* *days* for

For *a long time* the Israelites will dwell.

Hosea 3:4

Adverbial Accusative of Measure

This specifies the extent or measure associated with the verbal action.

וַיִּפֹּל מְלֹא־ קוֹמָתוֹ אַרְצָה

ground-toward *stature-his* *fullness-of* and-he-fell

He fell *full-length* to the ground.

1 Samuel 28:20

Prepositional Phrases (PP)

A prepositional phrase is a phrase that begins with a preposition. The preposition governs the other elements in the phrase. The governed elements comprise the OBJECT OF THE PREPOSITION. A prepositional phrase is thus a preposition and its object. Prepositional phrases in the predicate are adverbial elements not considered to be in the accusative case.

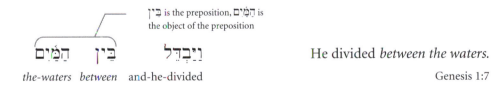

בֵּין is the preposition, הַמָּיִם is the object of the preposition

וַיַּבְדֵּל בֵּין הַמָּיִם

the-waters between and-he-divided

He divided *between the waters.*

Genesis 1:7

141

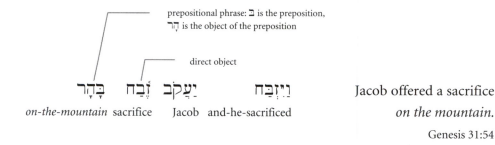

prepositional phrase: בְּ is the preposition,
הַר is the object of the preposition

direct object

בָּהָר   זֶ֫בַח   יַעֲקֹב   וַיִּזְבַּח

on-the-mountain sacrifice   Jacob   and-he-sacrificed

Jacob offered a sacrifice
on the mountain.

Genesis 31:54

142

SEMANTICS:
PROCESSES, ROLES, AND CIRCUMSTANCES

We use language to talk about the real world. Stop and think about it. Most everything we experience and understand about the phenomena of our existence we can represent in language, in its linguistic structures. The *semantic* concepts of **PROCESS**, **ROLE**, and **CIRCUMSTANCE** are categories we can use to help us see how the stuff of the real world meshes with language.[11]

By *process* we refer primarily to **VERBS**.

By *role* we refer primarily to **NOUNS/NOMINALS**.

By *circumstance* we refer primarily to **ADVERB(IAL)S** and **PREPOSITIONAL PHRASES**.

SEMANTIC PROCESSES

Though we can talk of others, we shall restrict ourselves to three *primary* semantic processes: (1) material, (2) mental, and (3) relational.

MATERIAL = DOING

The **MATERIAL** semantic process is the verbal process of **DOING**. Here a "*do-er*" has an impact on a "*do-ee*," so to speak. Quite often, the do-er is called the **AGENT** and the do-ee, the **PATIENT**. We can, however, be a little more precise. The *impact* a do-er can have is one of two things.

➢ **AFFECTOR—AFFECTED**

The do-er can **AFFECT** a do-ee. The do-er is the **AFFECTOR**, the do-ee is the **AFFECTED**. The affector and affected exist and the affector is the catalyst of an action that *affects* the existing affected.

---

[11] For further reading, see M.A.K. Halliday, *An Introduction to Functional Grammar* (2d ed.; London: Arnold, 1994), 109–60.

He hit *the idol.*

     Affector *(He)* — Affected *(the idol)*

Both the affector and affected already exist at the time of the verbal process, the hitting. The affector is the catalyst of the hitting that affects the affected.

> **EFFECTOR—EFFECTED**

The do-er can **EFFECT** a do-ee. The do-er is the **EFFECTOR**, the do-ee is the **EFFECTED**. The effector is the catalyst of an action that brings something into existence, the *effected.*

She built *the house.*

     Effector *(She)* — Effected *(the house)*

She grew *grapes.*

     Effector *(She)* — Effected *(grapes)*

The effector brings the effected into existence.

MENTAL = SENSING

The **MENTAL** semantic process is the verbal process of **SENSING**. Here a "**SENSE-ER**" has affection toward, cognition of, or uses the senses on a **PHE-NOMENON**. A senser is one who is able to feel (affection), to think (cognition), or to use the senses (see, hear, smell, etc.). A phenomenon is something about which a senser has feelings (affection), thoughts (cognition), or on which a senser has used the senses.

She loves *the man.*

     Senser *(She)* — Phenomenon *(the man)* = affection

He remembered *the story.*

Senser *(He)* — Phenomenon *(the story)* = cognition

Eli heard *Hannah's crying.*

Senser *(Eli)* — Phenomenon *(Hannah's crying)* = use of a sense

RELATIONAL = *BEING*

The **RELATIONAL** semantic process is the verbal process of **BEING**. We can talk of two types of relational processes.

➢ **CARRIER—ATTRIBUTE** = **ATTRIBUTIVE**

A **CARRIER** *carries* an **ATTRIBUTE.**

The book is *nonsense.*

Carrier *(The book)* — Attribute *(nonsense)*

The apple seems *green.*

Carrier *(The apple)* — Attribute *(green)*

The verbs tend to be an *ascriptive/descriptive* type. Here is a list of common verbs that convey an attributive semantic process.

become, turn (into), grow (into) = inception

remain, stay (as) = duration

seem, appear, qualify as, turn out, end up (as) = appearance

look, sound, smell, feel, taste (like) = sense-perception

be, feel = neutral

> ➢ **Identified—Identifier = Identifying**

An **IDENTIFIED** is assigned identity by an **IDENTIFIER**.

You are *the first person on earth.*

Identified *(You)* — Identifier *(the first person on earth)*

The verbs tend to be an *equative* type. Here is a list of common verbs that convey an identifying semantic process.

play, act as, function as, serve as = role

mean, indicate, suggest, imply, show, mark, reflect = sign

equal, add up to, make = equation

comprise, feature, include = kind/part

represent, constitute, form = significance

exemplify, illustrate = example

express, signify, realize, spell, stand for, mean = symbol

be, become, remain = neutral

Semantic Roles

We already have been talking about semantic **ROLES/PARTICIPANTS**. We have had to use this concept to talk about verbal processes in the last section. The concept of semantic roles or participants focuses on nouns/nominals in clauses and their relations to each other. We can divide roles/participants into those that occur as the syntactic subject of a clause and those that occur in the predicate. The chart below lists some common roles/participants in a clause.

Subject Roles	Predicate Roles
Affector	Affected
Effector	Effected
Senser	Phenomenon
Carrier	Attribute
Identified	Identifier
Processed	
	Beneficiary

In the previous section we saw examples of the roles listed in the first five rows. We need to understand the remaining roles.

Processed: role/participant that undergoes a process: *The apple* fell.

Beneficiary: role/participant as recipient of a benefit—positive or negative— from an action or a state/condition: He asked you for a favor *for himself.* I gave *him* the ball.

SEMANTIC CIRCUMSTANCES

Circumstances can surround verbal processes and roles/participants. English and Biblical Hebrew convey these circumstances primarily through adverb(ial)s and prepositional phrases. What follow are some of the common groupings of circumstances along with common structures used by English to convey the circumstance.

1) Circumstance of Extent (including interval)
   a) Distance (spatial)
      - structure: noun (with modifier): He traveled *many miles.*
   b) Duration (temporal)
      - structure: noun (with modifier): He slept *five days/a long time.*

2) Location
   a) Place (spatial)
      * structure: adverb: He lives *here/there.*
      * structure: prepositional phrase: He lives *in Galilee.*
   b) Time (temporal)
      * structure: adverb/noun (with modifier): He left *recently/a long time ago.*
      * structure: prepositional phrase: He left *at noon.*

3) Manner
   a) Means: means whereby a process takes place
      * structure: prepositional phrase: He fixed it *with rope.*
   b) Quality: characterizes the process
      * structure: adverbs: It rained *heavily.* She spoke *more calmly.*
   c) Comparison
      * structure: adverb: Aaron speaks *differently.*
      * structure: prepositional phrase: Her eyes are *like doves.*

4) Cause
   a) Reason: what causes a process
      * structure: prepositional phrase: *through, because of,* etc: They sang *because of the rain.*
   b) Purpose: intention behind a process
      * structure: prepositional phrase: *for, for the purpose of:* The gave up land *for peace.*
   c) Behalf: who is it for?
      * structure: prepositional phrase: *for, on behalf of:* I'm writing *for/on behalf of Jeremiah.*

5) Contingency
   a) Condition
      * structure: prepositional phrase: *in the case of, in the event of:* In the *event of* fire, use water.
      * structure: particle/conjunctions: *if, unless*

b) Concession: a circumstance conceded or granted or acknowledged
- structure: prepositional phrase: *in spite of*
- structure: particle/conjunctions: *although, though*

c) Default
- structure: prepositional phrase: *in the absence of*

6) Accompaniment

a) Comitative: a process represented as a single instance of a process
- Positive: *Moses and Aaron* went together. Moses went *with Aaron.* Moses set out *with his staff.*
- Negative: Moses went *without Aaron.* I got to the door *without my books.*

b) Additive: a process represented as two or more instances
- Positive: Moses went *as well as Aaron.*
- Negative: Moses went *instead of Aaron.*

7) Role

a) Guise: what as? He was confirmed *as High Priest.*

b) Product: what into? (what did it become?) He *became High Priest.* He *grew into a man.*

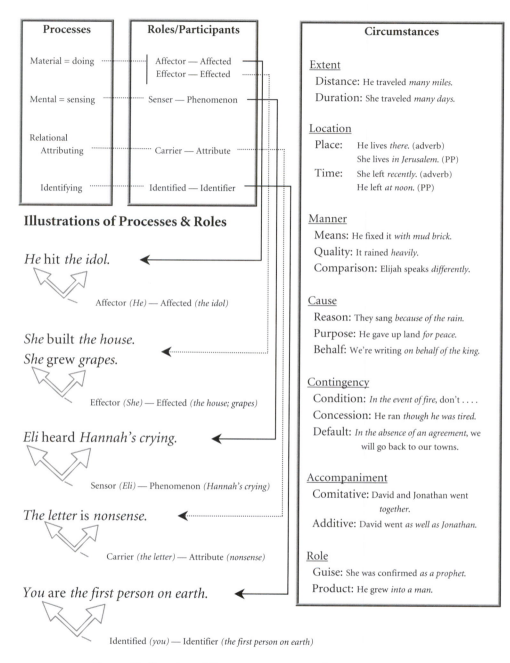

Processes	Roles/Participants
Material = doing	Affector — Affected
	Effector — Effected
Mental = sensing	Senser — Phenomenon
Relational	
Attributing	Carrier — Attribute
Identifying	Identified — Identifier

Circumstances

Extent
  Distance: He traveled *many miles*.
  Duration: She traveled *many days*.

Location
  Place: He lives *there*. (adverb)
       She lives *in Jerusalem*. (PP)
  Time: She left *recently*. (adverb)
       He left *at noon*. (PP)

Manner
  Means: He fixed it *with mud brick*.
  Quality: It rained *heavily*.
  Comparison: Elijah speaks *differently*.

Cause
  Reason: They sang *because of the rain*.
  Purpose: He gave up land *for peace*.
  Behalf: We're writing *on behalf of the king*.

Contingency
  Condition: *In the event of fire*, don't . . . .
  Concession: He ran *though he was tired*.
  Default: *In the absence of an agreement*, we
       will go back to our towns.

Accompaniment
  Comitative: David and Jonathan went
       together.
  Additive: David went *as well as Jonathan*.

Role
  Guise: She was confirmed *as a prophet*.
  Product: He grew *into a man*.

Illustrations of Processes & Roles

He hit *the idol*.

Affector *(He)* — Affected *(the idol)*

She built *the house*.
She grew *grapes*.

Effector *(She)* — Effected *(the house; grapes)*

Eli heard *Hannah's crying*.

Senser *(Eli)* — Phenomenon *(Hannah's crying)*

The letter is *nonsense*.

Carrier *(the letter)* — Attribute *(nonsense)*

You are *the first person on earth*.

Identified *(you)* — Identifier *(the first person on earth)*

Figure viii: Overview of Common Processes, Roles, and Circumstances

DISCOURSE ANALYSIS[12]

When we talk about **DISCOURSE** in linguistics, we are not usually referring to conversation or speech. The term refers more commonly to "chunks" of text and has in mind a level of language beyond looking at a clause isolated from another.

Discourse analysis, in short, takes seriously the notion of **CONTEXT**: (1) context in the one sense of the interrelation of words on a page, and (2) context in the sense of space and time—a language exchange or story-telling does not occur in a vacuum. More specifically, discourse analysis notices the interplay of story and discourse, concepts I discuss below. It tracks indicators of time, location, and what a text is *about,* that is, topicality. It takes note of what is an unmarked and marked way to write—more on that below. A little more technical definition is that discourse analysis is, in part, the interface of syntax, linguistic semantics, and linguistic pragmatics.

Take a look at a photograph of a family member or friend. You are looking at that person, but yet you are not. You are looking at a *representation.* Portraits present little trouble for us in that respect. We know that it represents a person though it is two-dimensional and not always true to life in size and color. We recognize that a self-portrait is not real. If poked, it will not yelp. If stabbed, it will not bleed.

Writing is representation. David and Goliath in the narrative writing known as 1 Samuel are not real people any more than a self-portrait of Vincent van Gogh is *really* or *actually* van Gogh. In saying that, however, I am not here judging whether David and Goliath actually existed any more than I am calling into question whether van Gogh really lived. David and Goliath in writing are not people, actual objects of genetics, but *personae,* objects of poetics and things linguistic. Discourse analysis understands that text is representation.

---

[12] Much of this chapter first appeared in my article "The Written Story: Toward Understanding Text as Representation and Function," *Vetus Testamentum* 49 (1999): 165–85.

1. STORY AND DISCOURSE

When it comes to representing, I have found it helpful to follow a distinction made by Seymour Chatman between STORY and DISCOURSE, whether representing through written page or cinema.[13]

If you were writing a novel, the *story* would be the conceptual content in your head—the plot, the characters, settings—before you wrote it down, and it would include the conceptual content that never gets written. The *discourse* of that novel, however, would be the actual book I pick up to read.

If we take a person's life, your life, for example, and somebody wanted to tell others about it in written form, the *story* of your life would begin at your birth and would go from there day by day. Story would be your actual life. The *discourse*—the words put onto a written page in this case—however, may begin by writing about what you are doing this moment, then flashback to various periods in your lifetime and rearrange them.

2. STORY HAPPENINGS AND DISCOURSE

The story, in the technical sense I am using it here, is developed, in part, by **HAPPENINGS**, that is, fientive events. When reading the Hebrew Bible (or any text), we should keep in mind that the discourse we are reading is only a representation of a story.

2.1 STORY-PRESENT, STORY-PAST, AND STORY-FUTURE

Discourse-level representation presents *perspective* I label STORY-PRESENT, STORY-PAST, and STORY-FUTURE. *Story-present* represents the happenings that are "at hand" in the discourse. Narrative *story-past* refers to perspective that is before the happenings that are "at hand" in the discourse. 1 Samuel 1 begins by describing happenings and STORY-EXISTENTS[14] that are anterior to the happenings that take

---

[13] Seymour Chatman, *Story and Discourse: Narrative Structure in Fiction and Film* (Ithaca, N.Y. and London: Cornell University Press, 1978).

[14] *Story-existents* are those story components that *exist:* settings, state-of-being, characters (apart from their actions), etc.

place on that one particular pilgrimage where Eli confronts Hannah, which is the story-present. Narrative *story-future* refers to perspective that is posterior to the "at hand" happenings. If, for example, I read, "Three years later Molly would discover that she had been speaking to her husband's murderer, but now she knew nothing," I have read story-future juxtaposed with story-present.

The discourse is free to rearrange the order of the actual story happenings—the present may be juxtaposed with its past or future—and is free to spend less or more time on a story happening than would be the time for a happening to occur in real life. Time relations of (1) order and (2) duration thus exist between story happenings and discourse.

2.2 ORDER

Discourse may rearrange story-happenings. The discourse preserved as Isaiah 36–39 does not chronologically follow the story happenings, the actual events. Chapters 36–37 center on Sennacherib's campaign in 701 B.C.E. while 38–39 center on Hezekiah's illness and a Babylonian envoy ca. 714–711 B.C.E.

2.3 DURATION

By *duration* I refer, following Chatman,[15] to the relation of the time it takes to read out a discourse compared to the time the story-happenings lasted or would last.

2.3.1 Summary

Duration may first be summary. Here, discourse is *significantly* briefer than story-time; it compresses story-time by days, weeks, months, years, and lifetimes. Genesis 4:17 reads, "Cain knew his wife, she conceived and bore Enoch; he built a city." You spent no more than five seconds to read something that would take a major part of a lifetime to achieve. Throughout the book of Kings one reads often a summary that a certain king ruled over Israel/Judah for a certain number of

---

[15] Chatman, *Story and Discourse,* 67–78.

years. Again, the discourse takes five seconds to read but represents a lifetime in *story*-time.

2.3.2 Ellipsis

In ellipsis discourse halts while story-time continues. Between Genesis 50:26 "Joseph died . . . and was embalmed and placed in a coffin in Egypt" and Exodus 1:8 "Now a new king arose over Egypt . . ." many story-happenings have been gapped. If we assume some historicity here for argument, Joseph could have attained his rank in the Delta under the Hyksos (Dynasty 15) or under lesser Asiatic dynasts (Dynasty 16). Hyksos influence seemingly extended from its apparent origins in the eastern Delta to the western half, where it dominated the Xioite Dynasty (14), advancing through a good portion of Egypt. Dissatisfaction among the Thebans with such a division of Egyptian kingship led to the eventual demise of the Hyksos, their expulsion being effected by Ahmose. With him the New Kingdom was established. The new king mentioned in Exodus likely belonged to this New Kingdom. None of these momentous events, known by every student of ancient Near Eastern history, is discoursed in the Bible.

2.3.3 Discourse-Time = Story-Time

In discourse-time = story-time, reading the discourse or text is approximate in time to what it would take for the actual situation. I mentioned above that summary representation *significantly* truncates story-time. Discourse-time = story-time, however, represents an almost precise match in time, in the case of dialogue between characters, or, at most, the compression of only a few moments.

2.3.4 Stretch

Stretch is where discourse-time is longer than story-time. In cinema this is slow motion. As an example in written discourse, we may look at Jael's killing of Sisera in the Deborah and Barak discourse preserved in Judges 4–5.

In the narrative portion, Judges 4:21, the writer represents the action in *discourse-time = story-time;* we read of Jael driving the tent peg through Sisera in the *approximate* amount of time as it may have taken in real life:

"But Jael wife of Heber took a tent peg, and took a hammer in her hand, and went quietly to him and drove the peg through his mouth[16] until it went down into the ground—he was lying fast asleep from weariness—and he died."

The poetic representation of this happening, found in Judges 5:26–27, is repetitive in relation to the narrative one:

"She put her hand to the tent peg and her right hand to the mallet; she hammered a blow to Sisera, she struck his head, she hit and pierced his (open) mouth. He sank, he fell, he lay still at her feet; at her feet he sank, he fell; where he sank, there he fell dead."

The discourse here, in a sense, is slower than the narrative representation. It is the written equivalent of cinematic slow motion; it is s-t-r-e-t-c-h-e-d.

2.3.5 Pause

In pause story-time stops but discourse continues. Here is where the writer describes people, scenes, and the like—things that are story-existents.

3. DISCOURSE AS THE FUNCTION OF SYNTAX, SEMANTICS, AND PRAGMATICS

When working with discourse you must realize that the functions of syntax, linguistic semantics, and pragmatics merge together in written representation. Truly grasping the conveyance of meaning comes by understanding the interrelation of these functions for a particular language.

Syntactic functions (Subject, Direct and Adverbial/Indirect Accusatives, etc.) articulate relationships and positions within a particular linguistic syntagm (that is, a string of words). *Semantic* functions specify, in part, the *meaning(s) of lexical items* (lexical semantics) and *roles* that referents may have (Agent, Patient, Goal, Manner, Instrument, Beneficiary, etc.). *Pragmatic* functions specify the

---

[16] The Hebrew word here translated as "mouth," which is usually translated "temple," is a rare and difficult word to understand; for "mouth" see M. Rozelaar, "An Unrecognized Part of the Human Anatomy," *Judaism* 37 (1988): 97–101, and Gary Long, "רַקָּה," in *New International Dictionary of Old Testament Theology and Exegesis* (ed. W. VanGemeren; 5 vols.; Grand Rapids, Mich.: Zondervan, 1997), 2:921–22.

informational status of part of a clause in relation to its wider contextual setting. This last function, pragmatics, affirms that natural language is carried out by humans in space and time. Language and language study, therefore, cannot be separated from humanity and human processes.

In the sub-sections that follow, I talk more about some of the major notions or ingredients that comprise discourse analysis.[17] In §3.4 below, we shall see these ingredients at work in specific examples.

3.1 TOPIC/TOPICALITY

A discourse is *about* something. It may, in fact, be about many things. This book, for example, is *about* basic grammatical concepts, this chapter is *about* discourse analysis, and this sub-section is *about* topicality. TOPIC or TOPICALITY in pragmatics considers what an expression may be about, whether that expression is a whole discourse or an individual clause.

We are really concerned here with COHERENCE, the conceptual or emic (see under LINGUISTIC HIERARCHIES, p. 3) notion of connectivity within a story and its discourse. Related to coherence is COHESION, a label that refers to the *physically present* (=etic) discourse features involved in bringing connectivity. For discourse to be coherent it must interface with REFERENCE FRAMES, any etic or conceptual (=emic) referent to which a discourse may refer. A reference frame may, in part, be real,[18] irreal,[19] physically present, or absent[20] in a discourse.

A discourse may have many referents or reference frames: one character, several characters, one happening, several happenings, etc. A reference frame may become a topic within a discourse. A coherent discourse must first introduce these

---

[17] For further reading, see Simon C. Dik, *The Theory of Functional Grammar, Part 1: The Structure of the Clause* (2d, revised ed.; ed. Kees Hengeveld; Functional Grammar Series 20; Berlin: Mouton de Gruyter, 1997).

[18] That is, a reference frame may refer to phenomena that are part of the world as we know it.

[19] That is, a reference frame may refer to imaginary phenomena.

[20] For example, the utterance "Please, start walking" may have a linguistically absent RF of people hurriedly wanting to leave a location.

topics—a **NEW** topic. Once a topic has been introduced and remains the topic, we can call it a **GIVEN** or **ACTIVE** topic. A topic that has not been mentioned for some time and is revived or re-introduced is a **RESUMED** topic.

3.2 FOCUS/FOCALITY

FOCUS or **FOCALITY,** another feature in pragmatics, attaches importance or saliency to a reference frame. A reference frame—usually a word or phrase—that is in *focus* is one that is informationally prominent or most salient.

3.3 MARKEDNESS

In language we need to talk, in part, of marked features and unmarked ones: **MARKEDNESS** and **UNMARKEDNESS**—elements that fall under the scope of linguistic pragmatics. If I say "Nehemiah examined Jerusalem on his mount" in normal intonation, I have likely expressed an *unmarked* English syntagm, that is, a string of words. The syntax, semantics, and pragmatic features of that expression are likely normal or most typical. If, however, I say "Nehemiah examined Jerusalem on his MOUNT" with high-falling intonation on "mount," I have expressed a *marked* syntagm, denoting that Nehemiah examined Jerusalem on *mount,* not by foot or by being carried. The syntax is the same. The semantic functions and meanings of the words are unchanged. The distinction between the two expressions, though, is a pragmatics feature. I could also say "On his MOUNT Nehemiah examined Jerusalem" with a change in syntax, the fronting of "on his mount" along with high intonation to mark the expression. We could in fact play that children's game of repeating the same expression while intonating a different word each time: NEHEMIAH examined Jerusalem on his mount; Nehemiah EXAMINED . . . ; Nehemiah examined JERUSALEM . . . ; etc. Each time you are expressing something meaningfully different.

Within discourse, markedness may be achieved, in part, through (1) quantity of information and (2) order or arrangement.[21]

---

[21] R. D. Bergen, "Text As a Guide to Authorial Intention: An Introduction to Discourse Criticism," *Journal of the Evangelical Theological Society* 30 (1987): 327–36.

3.3.1 Quantity of Information

Let us look first at quantity of information to denote markedness, and let us restrict ourselves here to written discourse. **QUANTITY**-markedness may be achieved syntactically by the length of a clause. Longer syntagms seem to be used for markedness in Exodus 12:29, while short, staccato-like clauses, too, may be used for markedness, particularly to mark a high point or climax of a story.

Within a large discourse, the overall length of a particular episode in relation to ones surrounding it may mark an atypical one within the immediate textual environment. The episode preserved as Genesis 1:24–31 is more than twice the length of each of the previous five;[22] that text calls out to us to say, "I am marked, I am particularly important." An important factor in deriving what is likely quantity-marked in a particular textual environment is taking note of what seems to be common in the immediate textual environment.

3.3.2 Order of Information

ORDER-markedness may be achieved, in one way, through word order in clauses—syntax. The narrator's "voice," so to speak, or *narrator's frame* in Biblical Hebrew **PAST-TIME NARRATIVE** shows two main, root, or non-subordinating syntactic clause types:

➤ clauses initiated with *vav*-consecutive plus Prefix (Imperfect) Conjugation—*vayyiqtol* clauses;

➤ clauses *not* initiated with *vav*-consecutive plus Prefix (Imperfect) Conjugation—non-*vayyiqtol* clauses.

Keep in mind that we are talking now only about a narrow, but heavily used, genre, past-time narrative, and, within that genre, only about the narrator's frame. **VAYYIQTOL** and **NON-VAYYIQTOL** seem to be the broadest and most helpful labels for Biblical Hebrew under which we can subsume all the syntactic phenomena within the past-time narrator's frame.

---

[22] Genesis 1:1–5 (52 words); 1:6–8 (38 words); 1:9–13 (69 words); 1:14–19 (69 words); 1:20–23 (57 words). Genesis 1:24–31 has 149 words.

The *vayyiqtol* clause appears to be the linguistically unmarked or normative clausal structure that, in general, pushes along the plot. The non-*vayyiqtol* clause appears to be a marked syntagm. Markedness, though, may have a higher or lower value depending on the overall frequency of what is identified as a marked pattern. Within Jonah, excluding the poem (2:3–10), non-*vayyiqtol* clauses comprise only 8% of the main clauses within the narrator's frame. Within the narrator's frame of the past-time narrative portions of the Joseph discourse (Genesis 37–50), only 22% of main clauses are non-*vayyiqtol*. The low occurrence of non-*vayyiqtol* syntagms in those texts affirms the markedness status of the non-*vayyiqtol* syntagms in those particular texts. In a discourse where the ratio would approach parity with the *vayyiqtol*, the markedness value of the non-*vayyiqtol* should likely be considered quite diminished. One must be sensitive to the data to be discovered in a given discourse.

One must look carefully for markedness and unmarkedness in text. What I am saying in practice then is that noting the constituent(s) at the beginning of clauses, is, in part, vitally important for perceiving order-markedness within and among main clauses. I shall return to this below under §4.

3.4 MARKEDNESS FOR FOCUS AND CONNECTIVITY

Markedness may convey pragmatic FOCUS, again, the salient or prominent pragmatic information in a clause. It also plays an important role in a discourse's connectivity (coherence and cohesion). Sometimes a discourse, within its clausal structures, marks a clausal element or constituent that serves as a reference frame for guiding the Recipient in tracking how clauses cohere or are grouped together:

a)   Nehemiah examined Jerusalem on his mount.

b)   On his mount Nehemiah examined Jerusalem.

In both (a) and (b) the notion 'mount' is a reference frame (as is 'Nehemiah', 'Jerusalem', 'examine', plus potentially a host of absent reference frames). In (a) the reference frame represented in the phrase "on his mount" is unmarked, syntactically being placed in a normative position for English and without stressed intonation. In (b), however, the reference frame, represented in a *fronted* position within the clause, is marked. A **MARKED COHESION REFERENCE FRAME** (MCRF) is a label to refer to this kind of marked clausal constituent. Since a reference frame may or may not be explicitly mentioned in a discourse, the use of *cohesion* in the label refers to a reference frame being a linguistic constituent explicitly mentioned in the discourse.

These notions of focus and MCRF are here illustrated:

➢ Nehemiah examined Jerusalem on his mount.

The last example was unmarked; it was normative English. All the following examples, however, are marked in some way.

➢ Nehemiah examined Jerusalem on his MOUNT [focus]. [high-falling intonation on "mount" to mark prominent information]

➢ It was ON HIS MOUNT [focus] that Nehemiah examined Jerusalem. [cleft clause construction and high intonation to mark prominent information]

➢ ON HIS MOUNT [focus] Nehemiah examined Jerusalem. [fronting of the prepositional phrase and high intonation to mark prominent information]

➢ On his mount [MCRF] Nehemiah examined Jerusalem. [normal intonation on fronted prepositional phrase; the fronted phrase—a marked construction—could here be presenting MCRF; Nehemiah's mount could have been mentioned previously and is important somehow for discourse coherence apart from being particularly prominent]

➢ On his MOUNT [focus + MCRF overlay] Nehemiah examined Jerusalem. [fronting of the prepositional phrase and high intonation to mark prominent information (as in the previous example), plus a speaker or writer might want to convey MCRF, Nehemiah's mount could have been mentioned previously and is important somehow for discourse coherence]

3.4.1 Types of Focus[23]

Focus refers to the salient or prominent pragmatic information in a clause. It concerns the changes that a Sender (speaker or writer) wants to make in the Recipient's pragmatic information. Focus can be achieved, as I demonstrated in part in the preceding section, through (a) prosody (e.g., intonation), (b) syntax, whether a special initial position within a clause or a special syntactic construction (e.g., a cleft construction), and (c) special Focus marking words or particles.

In using Focus the Sender may want to (1) fill in an assumed gap of information or (2) make a contrast. The first, INFORMATION GAP FOCUS, may entail

(1a) *Questioning Focus,* where the Sender will ask a question:

What did you do to Jerusalem's walls? [focus marked with wh- interrogative construction]

(1b) *Completive Focus,* where the Sender attempts to fill-in an assumed information gap:

I REPAIRED them. [focus marked with intonation]

CONTRAST FOCUS may comprise

(2a) *Parallel Focus,* which usually highlights simultaneous or concurrent phenomena:

The Philistines prepared for war; SAUL and the ISRAELITES also prepared for battle.

(2b) *Counter-Presuppositional Focus,* which embraces several more specific functions:

(2bi) *Rejecting Focus:* not A!; David killed Ammonites. No, he didn't kill AMMONITES.

(2bii) *Replacing Focus:* (not A, but) B; David killed Ammonites. No, he killed JEBUSITES.

---

[23] For further reading, see Dik, *Theory of Functional Grammar,* 309–38.

161

(2biii)   *Expanding Focus:* also B; David killed Ammonites. He not only killed AMMONITES, he killed JEBUSITES.

(2biv)   *Restricting Focus:* only B; David killed Ammonites and Jebusites. No, he killed only JEBUSITES.

(2bv)   *Selecting Focus:* (A or B) B!; Did David kill Ammonites or Jebusites? JEBUSITES.

3.4.2 Types of MCRFs

An MCRF, by definition, is a reference frame that is pragmatically marked. A **NewMCRF** introduces a new referent. Once a referent has been introduced and finds itself marked it can be considered **GivenMCRF** or **ActiveMCRF**. **ResumptiveMCRF** refers to a referent that has not been mentioned for some time and is revived or re-introduced in a marked fashion.

4. A MARKEDNESS APPROACH TO BIBLICAL HEBREW PAST-TIME NARRATIVE

In a *written* text where we have no oral clues or other modern conventions such as capital letters, bold, or italics (which I have likely overused in this chapter), the beginning of a clause is vitally important as one way of perceiving markedness within and among main clauses. I have started by observing clause-level syntactic phenomena. These observations have informed what I have concluded about their functions at the discourse-level. Form and function ever interact.

An interpreter of any text, and especially of the Bible, needs to bring this aspect of investigation into the process. Understanding how a discourse brings something into focus or tracks topics goes to the core of deriving meaning from a text. It ought to be a foundation of exegesis. Basic translation, in fact, needs to convey these meaningful elements appropriately.

4.1 THE VAYYIQTOL

4.1.1 The *vayyiqtol* as Unmarked Mainline

When, and it is hardly always the case, but *when* the *vayyiqtol* clause denotes happenings and pushes along the narrative plot, I consider the label MAINLINE of the story useful. The label mainline seems to describe appropriately the *vayyiqtol* clause's common function of pushing along an episode and, more broadly, a plot. *Vayyiqtol* mainline may represent a variety of happening-types. I highlight three as illustrative.

4.1.1.1 Mainline Linear/Subsequent Happenings

The plot may be pushed along by happenings expressed in a linear or subsequent fashion, i.e., action A, then action B, then action C, and on like that. The subsequence may be either temporal or logical. For example, 1 Samuel 17:49.

49a			וַיִּשְׁלַח דָּוִד אֶת־יָדוֹ אֶל־הַכֶּלִי
	the-bag	to DO-hand-his David and-he-sent

49b		וַיִּקַּח מִשָּׁם אֶבֶן
	stone from-there then-he-took

49c	וַיְקַלַּע
	then-he-slung

49d			וַיַּךְ אֶת־הַפְּלִשְׁתִּי אֶל־מִצְחוֹ
	brow-his	to DO-the-Philistine then-he-struck

David put his hand into the shepherd's bag and took out a stone. He hurled it with a sling and struck the Philistine on his brow. 1 Samuel 17:49

4.1.1.2 Mainline Cluster Happenings

Not all mainline, of course, is linear or subsequent. Two or more *vayyiqtol* clauses may cluster with a view to a single happening. One particular type concerns the Biblical Hebrew verbal roots that, while being *syntactically* analyzable as *vayyiqtol*s in main clauses and initiating a mainline clause, seem, *semantically* to modify or offer a comment on a following *vayyiqtol*: וַיֹּסֶף, וַיְמַהֵר, וַיָּשָׁב, וַיַּשְׁכֵּם, etc. Consider, for example, the following clauses.

וַיֹּסֶף אַבְרָהָם

Abraham and-he-added

וַיִּקַּח אִשָּׁה

woman and-he-took

Abraham married another woman. Genesis 25:1

Such syntagms particularly highlight the difficulty of defining the concept of *clause*, to say nothing of *sentence*, in Biblical Hebrew. Should we say that the syntagm וַיֹּסֶף אַבְרָהָם וַיִּקַּח אִשָּׁה is two independent/root clauses or one complex/extended clause?

4.1.1.3 Mainline Simultaneous Happenings

Two or more *vayyiqtol* clauses may represent nearly simultaneous happenings. For example, Genesis 45:2:

2a   וַיִּתֵּן אֶת־קֹלוֹ בִּבְכִי

in-crying DO-voice-his and-he-gave

2b   וַיִּשְׁמְעוּ מִצְרַיִם

Egyptians and-they-heard

2c   וַיִּשְׁמַע בֵּית פַּרְעֹה

Pharaoh house-of and-it-heard

He [Joseph] cried so loudly that the Egyptians heard him and the news got as far as Pharaoh's palace. Genesis 45:2

4.1.2 The *vayyiqtol* as Sideline/Exposition

The *vayyiqtol* commonly functions to discourse a story's mainline, yet it may also denote something we can label SIDELINE or EXPOSITION. In written etic discourse, which is, after all, a linear string of syntagms, one may need to "break off" in order to "enflesh" a character, describe a setting, etc. Such discourse interruption clearly aligns itself with the nature of the broad phenomenon known as *exposition* in plot development. In Biblical Hebrew past-time narrative, it continually interjects into the plot. The episode concerning Jericho, Rahab, and the spies offers insight.

3a   וַיִּשְׁלַח מֶלֶךְ יְרִיחוֹ אֶל־רָחָב לֵאמֹר

      saying   Rahab   to   Jericho   king-of   and-he-sent

3b   "..." (Direct Speech)

4a   וַתִּקַּח הָאִשָּׁה אֶת־שְׁנֵי הָאֲנָשִׁים

      the-men   DO-two-of   the-woman   and-she-took

4b   וַתִּצְפְּנוֹ

      and-she-hid-him

4c   וַתֹּאמֶר

      and-she-said

4d   "..." (Direct Speech)

5   "..." (Direct Speech continues)

6a   וְהִיא הֶעֱלָתַם הַגָּגָה

      the-roof-toward   she-took-them   and-she

→ 6b   וַתִּטְמְנֵם בְּפִשְׁתֵּי הָעֵץ הָעֲרֻכוֹת לָהּ עַל־הַגָּג

      the-roof   on   by-her   the-arranged   the-stalks   in-flax-of   and-she-hid-them

[3]The king of Jericho sent an order to Rahab, "...." [4]The woman had taken the two men and had hidden them. She replied, "...." [6]*Now she herself had taken them up to the roof <u>and had hidden them in the flax stalks arranged by her on the roof.</u>* Joshua 2:3–6

Clause 6b, initiated by a *vayyiqtol,* seems hardly to function on the mainline. The clause rather describes a happening after the happening described in 6a, a non-*vayyiqtol* exposition clause (see §4.2.2.1.1 below), seemingly marked for *Completive Focus* or *Selecting Focus* with *GivenMCRF* overlay (since Rahab is speaking just prior to 6a)—"Now <u>SHE</u> herself had taken them up ... and had hidden them ...." High intonation falls on הִיא "she." The translation I offer tries to convey the same meaning of the markedness of the Hebrew (by using "now" and "herself," plus the high intonation).

Another example, though less certain, is in v.4. This verse seems to be an initial reference to the hiding-happening in v.6, which we just considered. The king has sent a message to Rahab. As we read v.3b, are we reading along in the discourse at a point when the message is being read directly to Rahab or are we simply being informed of the contents of the message? If the king's officials are conveying the message directly to Rahab in v.3b, then her response is reported in v.4d–5. The clauses 4a–b, then, could be understood as representing a story-past happening (note RSV "But the woman *had taken* the two men and *hidden* them" [emphasis mine]); they could be here functioning as *vayyiqtol* as sideline/exposition. The direct speech in v.3, however, could represent the officials' message outside Rahab's dwelling, before a face-to-face encounter, Rahab simultaneously scrambling to hide the spies before replying. More certain is that the hiding-happening, which likely functions as sideline or exposition, is conveyed in an unmarked fashion in v.4a–b, while the same happening begins with marked representation in v.6a.

4.2 THE NON-VAYYIQTOL

I said earlier that the non-*vayyiqtol* clause appears to be a marked construction, in part, for focus and/or MCRF phenomena. The clause-type may push along the plot or, more commonly, interrupt it, as it were.

4.2.1 The Non-*vayyiqtol* as Marked Mainline

I believe mainline is perhaps best traced through the **FIENTIVE** happenings, that is, happenings that convey action, activity, and dynamism. The non-*vayyiqtol* marked mainline, then, is likely to be found represented by **X-QATAL** clauses, that is, clauses that begin with something other than a verb then followed by a fientive Suffix (Perfect) Conjugation verb (referred to as *qatal*). 1 Samuel 17:1–2 is illustrative.

1a	וַיַּאַסְפוּ פְלִשְׁתִּים אֶת־מַחֲנֵיהֶם לַמִּלְחָמָה	
	for-the-battle DO-camps-their Philistines and-they-assembled	
1b	וַיֵּאָסְפוּ שֹׂכֹה אֲשֶׁר לִיהוּדָה	
	to-Judah which Socoh and-they-were-assembled	
1c	וַיַּחֲנוּ בֵּין שׂוֹכֹה וּבֵין עֲזֵקָה בְּאֶפֶס דַּמִּים	
	Dammim in-Efes Azeqah and-between Socoh between and-they-camped	
→ 2a	וְשָׁאוּל וְאִישׁ־יִשְׂרָאֵל נֶאֶסְפוּ	
	they-assembled Israel and-man-of and-Saul	

166

2b	הָאֵלָה	בְּעֵמֶק		וַיַּחֲנוּ
	the-Elah	in-valley-of		and-they-camped

2c	מִלְחָמָה לִקְרַאת פְּלִשְׁתִּים			וַיַּעַרְכוּ
	Philistines to-meet battle			and-they-arranged

The Philistines prepared for war. They assembled against Socoh, which belonged to Judah, camping at Efes-Dammim between Socoh and Azeqah. *Saul and Israel's army gathered, too,* set up camp at Elah Valley, and drew up battle lines opposite the Philistine army. 1 Samuel 17:1–2

Clause 2a, though non-*vayyiqtol*, hardly functions as story exposition or sideline. Notice formally that 2a is X-*qatal* in a textual environment of five fientive *vayyiqtol* clauses. Here the non-*vayyiqtol* clause 2a in an X-*qatal* format seems to mark focus and MCRF phenomena. Clause 2a likely functions as *Parallel Focus,* the parallel actions of Saul and the army being made particularly salient juxtaposed to what the Philistines were doing. As for textual coherence, if one looks only at this particular episode initiated at 17:1, clause 2a introduces *NewMCRF*— Saul is being newly introduced into this particular episode, which has ear-marks of being more originally a self-contained story. If we keep the broader canonical story in mind, Saul, as a character, is being reactivated, *ResumptiveMCRF.* Clause 2a likely denotes MCRF with focus overlay. Aurally, we might have heard high intonation from an ancient reader or storyteller on וְשָׁאוּל וְאִישׁ־יִשְׂרָאֵל "SAUL and ISRAEL'S ARMY."

The two main clauses in Joshua 2:7 comprise two further examples:

→7a	הַמַּעְבְּרוֹת עַל הַיַּרְדֵּן דֶּרֶךְ אַחֲרֵיהֶם רָדְפוּ			וְהָאֲנָשִׁים
	the-fords to the-Jordan way-of after-them they-pursued			and-the-men

→7b	אַחֲרֵיהֶם הָרֹדְפִים יָצְאוּ כַּאֲשֶׁר אַחֲרֵי סָגְרוּ			וְהַשַּׁעַר
	after-them the-pursuers they-exited when after they-closed			and-the-gate

So those men pursued them along the Jordan road toward the fords. The gate was then closed as soon as the pursuit-group left. Joshua 2:7

The markedness of clause 7a, where the reference frame 'men', represented by the word הָאֲנָשִׁים, is placed before the fientive Suffix (Perfect) Conjugation verb, appears to convey *ActiveMCRF*. The syntactic direct object הַשַּׁעַר placed before the fientive Suffix (Perfect) Conjugation verb in clause 7b likely conveys a type of focus more than an MCRF, though a 'closed gate' reference frame could lend connectivity to why, in part, the spies leave the city through a window (v.15).

4.2.2 The Non-*vayyiqtol* as Sideline/Exposition

The non-*vayyiqtol* is more commonly the stuff of sideline or exposition. I think maintaining that non-*vayyiqtol* exposition may reflect (1) action and (2) non-action is helpful.

4.2.2.1 The Non-*vayyiqtol* as Sideline/Exposition *Action*

Exposition that reflects action and activity is presented in at least three different syntactic arrangements: (1) X–V clauses, (2) verb-initial clauses, and (3) verbless clauses with predicate participles (see the section **PREDICATE FUNCTION**, p. 79, under **PARTICIPLE**). The verbal forms denote fientivity.

4.2.2.1.1 X–V Clauses

Clauses are commonly X–V (words that are not verbs followed by a verb) with the clause containing a fientive verbal form.

4c	מֵחָרָן בְּצֵאתוֹ שָׁנָה וְשִׁבְעִים שָׁנִים חָמֵשׁ בֶּן־ וְאַבְרָם
	from-Haran in-exiting-his year and-seventy years five son-of and-Abram

Now Abram was seventy-five years old when he *left* Haran. Genesis 12:4

We may revisit Joshua 2:6, cited above under §4.1.2, where attention was on v.6b. Clause 6a, though, is an X–V clause containing a fientive Suffix (Perfect) Conjugation, וְהִיא הֶעֱלָתַם הַגָּגָה, "Now she herself had taken them up to the roof." Its function is to provide story-past information, telling the reader what Rahab herself had done likely before she ever began talking with the officials.

4.2.2.1.2 Verb-Initial Clauses

Clauses can be verb-initial, where the verbal form is a *vav*-consecutive + fientive Suffix (Perfect) Conjugation.

vav-consecutive +
Suffix (Perfect) Conjugation

→ 3a וְעָלָה הָאִישׁ הַהוּא מֵעִירוֹ מִיָּמִים יָמִ֫ימָה

and-he-goes-up the-man the-that from-city-his from-days days-toward

לְהִשְׁתַּחֲוֺת וְלִזְבֹּחַ לַיהוה צְבָאוֹת בְּשִׁלֹה

to-worship and-to-sacrifice to-YHWH hosts in-Shiloh

3b וְשָׁם שְׁנֵי בְנֵי־עֵלִי חָפְנִי וּפִנְחָס כֹּהֲנִים לַיהוה

and-there two-of sons-of Eli Hophni and-Pinhas priests to-YHWH

4a וַיְהִי הַיּוֹם

and-it-was the-day

4b וַיִּזְבַּח אֶלְקָנָה

and-he-sacrificed Elqanah

→ 4c וְנָתַן לִפְנִנָּה אִשְׁתּוֹ וּלְכָל־בָּנֶיהָ וּבְנוֹתֶיהָ מָנוֹת

and-he-gives to-Peninnah wife-his and-to-all sons-her and-daughters-her portions

5a וּלְחַנָּה יִתֵּן מָנָה אַחַת אַפָּ֫יִם (subordinate כִּי clause +) . . . (?)

and-to-Hannah he-gives portion one . . . (?)

That man *would/used to go up* from his town regularly on pilgrimages to
worship and sacrifice to YHWH of hosts at Shiloh, where Eli's two sons, Hophni and Pinhas, were serving as priests to YHWH. When the particular day
came [on each pilgrimage] for Elqanah to offer a sacrifice, *he used to give* a
portion each to his wife Peninnah and to all her sons and daughters. To
Hannah, however, he would give a double(?)/half(?) portion . . . . 1 Samuel
1:3a–5a

Clauses 3a and 4c are initiated with *vav*-consecutive + fientive Suffix (Perfect)
Conjugation verbs. These clauses express habitual aspect in story-past, which is
distinct here from a mainline. Notice that clause 5a, with its fientive Prefix (Imperfect) Conjugation continuing the habitual aspect denoted in 4c, serves as another example of non-*vayyiqtol* X–V for sideline/exposition action (see
§4.2.2.1.1).

4.2.2.1.3 Verbless Clauses

Clauses can contain participles that convey fientivity. A participle is commonly
used as a predicator in a *verbless* clause. Though this **PREDICATE PARTICIPLE** (see

169

the section **PREDICATE FUNCTION**, p. 79, under **PARTICIPLE**) in Biblical Hebrew
seems to approximate the *function* of a finite verb, a clause with a predicate participle is nevertheless considered verbless.

Qal active participle

3a   מִזֶּה   אֶל־הָהָר   עֹמְדִים   וּפְלִשְׁתִּים

from-this   the-mountain   to   *standing*   and-Philistines

3b   מִזֶּה   אֶל־הָהָר   עֹמְדִים   וְיִשְׂרָאֵל

from-this   the-mountain   to   *standing*   and-Israel

The Philistines occupied the high ground on one side and the Israelites occupied the high ground on the other. 1 Samuel 17:3a–b

Admittedly, one could argue that "standing" may not be very *action*-oriented.
That may well be true. I have, however, kept the *form* of the participle and the
textual environment in mind. It is a Qal active participle, which commonly conveys fientivity, as distinct from Qal stative participles (for notions of *fientivity* and
stativity see the section **FIENTIVE AND STATIVE**, p. 85, under **VERB**). My
translation of an army *occupying* a position tries to convey the fientivity and dynamism entailed in maintaining a strategic battle position.

4.2.2.2 The Non-*vayyiqtol* as Sideline/Exposition *Non-Action*

Exposition that reflects non-action and/or setting is presented, in part, as (1)
verbless and (2) X–V, where the verbal form is stative.

4.2.2.2.1 Verbless Clauses

2a   נָשִׁים   שְׁתֵּי   וְלוֹ

women   two-of   and-to-him

2b   חַנָּה   אַחַת   שֵׁם

Hannah   one   name-of

2c   פְּנִנָּה   הַשֵּׁנִית   וְשֵׁם

Peninnah   the-second   and-name-of

He [Elqanah] had two wives, one named Hannah, the other Peninnah.
1 Samuel 1:2a–c

4.2.2.2.2 X–V Clauses

X–V clauses contain a stative verbal noun or stative Suffix (Perfect) Conjugation.

11a
stative participle =
verbal adjective

זְקֵנִים   וְשָׂרָה   וְאַבְרָהָם

old   and-Sarah   and-Abraham

Now Abraham and Sarah were old. Genesis 18:11

10a
Suffix (Perfect) Conjugation

מִזֹּקֶן   כָּבְדוּ   יִשְׂרָאֵל   וְעֵינֵי

from-old-age   *they-were-heavy*   Israel   and-eyes-of

Now Israel's eyes were dim from old age. Genesis 48:10

5. ILLUSTRATION

As an illustration for trying to apply these insights to a text, I have broken down the discourse of 1 Samuel 17:1–3 into main clauses including dependent/subordinate clauses associated with the main clause. Remember, this is past-time narrative. We are not considering any other type of text (speech, poetry, etc.) at the moment.

TEXT, 17:1a	לַמִּלְחָמָה אֶת־מַחֲנֵיהֶם פְּלִשְׁתִּים וַיַּאַסְפוּ
GLOSS	for-the-war DO-camps-their Philistines and-they-gathered
TRANSLATION	The Philistines prepared for war.
INITIAL POSITION	*vayyiqtol* = *vav* + Prefix (Imperfect) Conjugation
COMMENTARY	• Unmarked mainline = §4.1.1 above; this clause is likely a discourse-opening mainline statement the offers the "big picture," as it were.

TEXT, 17:1b	לִיהוּדָה אֲשֶׁר שֹׂכֹה וַיֵּאָסְפוּ
GLOSS	to-Judah which Socoh and-they-assembled(-themselves)

171

TRANSLATION They assembled at Socoh in Judah,

INITIAL POSITION *vayyiqtol* = *vav* + Prefix (Imperfect) Conjugation

COMMENTARY • Unmarked mainline = §4.1.1 above.

• The *happening* of 'assemble', which the verb conveys, may be a separate happening *subsequent* to the previous clause, 17:1a; see §4.1.1.1 above.

• The *happening* of 'assemble', however, may have the same happening in mind and thus be mainline *cluster* happening; see §4.1.1.2 above.

TEXT, 17:1c וַיֵּחָנוּ בֵּין־ שׂוֹכֹה וּבֵין־ עֲזֵקָה בְּאֶפֶס דַּמִּים:

GLOSS and-they-camped between Socoh and-between Azeqah in-Efes Dammim

TRANSLATION camping at Efes-Dammim between Socoh and Azeqah.

INITIAL POSITION *vayyiqtol* = *vav* + Prefix (Imperfect) Conjugation

COMMENTARY • Unmarked mainline = §4.1.1 above.

• The happening of 'camp' could either be a happening *subsequent* to assembling together (§4.1.1.1 above) or part of a *cluster* of happenings (§4.1.1.2 above) that are not necessarily precisely subsequent.

TEXT, 17:2a וְשָׁאוּל וְאִישׁ־ יִשְׂרָאֵל נֶאֶסְפוּ

GLOSS and-Saul and-man-of Israel they-assembled

TRANSLATION Saul and Israel's army gathered, too,

INITIAL POSITION Non-*vayyiqtol*

COMMENTARY • Marked mainline, X-*qatal* = §4.2.1 above; that is, this is a clause that *begins* with something other than a verb but does contain a Suffix (Perfect) Conjugation in the clause.

• Parallel focus: I highlighted this clause in §4.2.1 above. The parallel actions of Saul and the army are being made particularly salient juxtaposed to what the Philistines were doing at the same time. See more under §3.4.1 above.

• NewMCRF: Saul and the army are being newly introduced in a marked fashion into this particular episode initiated

172

at 17:1. If we keep the broader canonical perspective in mind, however, Saul and the army, as characters, are being reactivated into the discourse in a marked fashion, ResumptiveMCRF. See above at §3.4.2.

TEXT, 17:2b	וַֽיַּחֲנוּ בְּעֵמֶק הָאֵלָה
GLOSS	the-Elah in-valley-of and-they-camped
TRANSLATION	set up camp at Elah Valley,
INITIAL POSITION	*vayyiqtol* = *vav* + Prefix (Imperfect) Conjugation
COMMENTARY	• Unmarked mainline = §4.1.1 above.

• After the previous clause, which had a *marked* construction, the discourse goes back to an unmarked mainline format to represent the happening.

• The happening of 'camp' could either be a happening *subsequent* to assembling together, which was expressed in a marked fashion in 17:2a or part of a *cluster* of happenings (§4.1.1.2 above) that are not necessarily precisely subsequent.

TEXT, 17:2c	וַיַּֽעַרְכוּ מִלְחָמָה לִקְרַאת פְּלִשְׁתִּים:
GLOSS	Philistines to-meet battle and-they-arranged
TRANSLATION	and drew up battle lines opposite the Philistine army.
INITIAL POSITION	*vayyiqtol* = *vav* + Prefix (Imperfect) Conjugation
COMMENTARY	• Unmarked mainline = §4.1.1 above.

• The happening of 'arrange' is likely a happening *subsequent* to setting up camp, the happening in 17:2b (see §4.1.1.1 above).

TEXT, 17:3a	וּפְלִשְׁתִּים עֹמְדִים אֶל־הָהָר מִזֶּה
GLOSS	from-this the-mountain to standing and-Philistines
TRANSLATION	Now the Philistines occupied the high ground on one side
INITIAL POSITION	Non-*vayyiqtol*
COMMENTARY	• Marked construction of non-*vayyiqtol* as sideline/exposition = §4.2.2 above.

173

- The discourse breaks off from mainline fientive happenings to help describe the setting.
- Above I analyzed this clause as non-*vayyiqtol* as sideline/exposition action expressed through a verbless clause (see §4.2.2.1.3 above).
- ResumptiveMCRF: Saul and the army have been the syntactic subject and the topic of the previous clause. The *Philistines* are reintroduced as the topic into the discourse in a marked way.

TEXT, 17:3b	מִזֶּה אֶל־הָהָר עֹמְדִים וְיִשְׂרָאֵל
GLOSS	from-this the-mountain to standing and-Israel
TRANSLATION	while Israel occupied the high ground on the other.
INITIAL POSITION	Non-*vayyiqtol*
COMMENTARY	

- Marked construction of non-*vayyiqtol* as sideline/exposition = §4.2.2 above.
- Above I analyzed this clause as non-*vayyiqtol* as sideline/exposition action expressed through a verbless clause (see §4.2.2.1.3 above).
- Parallel focus: Israel's position is made particularly salient in relation to the Philistines.
- ResumptiveMCRF: *Israel* is reintroduced as the grammatical subject and topic of this clause.

TEXT, 17:3c	בֵּינֵיהֶם: וְהַגַּיְא
GLOSS	between-them and-the-valley
TRANSLATION	The valley lay between them.
INITIAL POSITION	Non-*vayyiqtol*
COMMENTARY	

- Marked construction of non-*vayyiqtol* as sideline/exposition non-action expressed through a verbless clause = §4.2.2.2.1 above.
- Focus: the valley (הַגַּיְא) is prominent or salient information.

- NewMCRF: the valley, into which Goliath struts daily and in which David eventually kills Goliath is introduced into the text.

6. CONCLUDING REMARK

I have treated the Hebrew Bible text, as do most discourse analysts, in its final form—as though one person sat down and penned precisely what is there. But this is hardly how our texts came to be. Biblical texts are a tension of unity, diversity, and complexity.

Source Critics may look at "final form"-oriented approaches and understandably cry "foul!" The texts, after all, are diachronic and heavily reliant on sources. How can one be certain that a particular feature is markedness in discourse (or whatever) and not simply a stitch, a seam between sources?

The short answer is that no one can be certain. The text of the Hebrew Bible is complex in its origin and development. This necessitates that discourse analysts hedge what we say about "final-form" phenomena. Prudence dictates acknowledging that a join or a seam may ultimately be behind what is labeled a particular discourse feature.

At the same time, however, if one may admit that a given text of the Hebrew Bible is a worked-over piece derived from multi-sources over generations of time, one may also admit that it is indeed *worked-over*. No one should think it ludicrous to expect texts so central and core to the very fabric of a people-group, in the final analysis, to be put together well—to communicate well according to the conventions of the literary language we call Biblical Hebrew.

Here I find insight from a text like the Mesha inscription, which I have analyzed, in part, in my *Vetus Testamentum* article. Multi-sources behind the inscription's final text are likely not part of the equation to the degree they are for the Hebrew Bible. The text tells a story in the conventions of the Moabite literary language of the day it was written and the text has remained the same for millennia. What is fascinating is that one seems to find similar, if not precisely some of the same discourse phenomena of the Hebrew Bible text. This ancient text that comes directly from antiquity and so closely parallels Hebrew Bible textual phenomena can argue that Hebrew Bible text, in the final analysis, has been well put together in its language medium.

Like a photograph, writing is representation. We have looked in cursory fashion at story and discourse and how the blend of syntax, semantics, and pragmatics must inform your analysis of text.

WORKS CITED

Barnwell, Katharine. *Introduction to Semantics and Translation.* 2d ed. Horsley Green, England: Summer Institute of Linguistics, 1980.

Bergen, R. D. "Text As a Guide to Authorial Intention: An Introduction to Discourse Criticism." *Journal of the Evangelical Theological Society* 30 (1987): 327–36.

Chatman, Seymour. *Story and Discourse: Narrative Structure in Fiction and Film.* Ithaca, N.Y. and London: Cornell University Press, 1978.

Cook, John A. "The Biblical Hebrew Verbal System: A Grammaticalization Approach." Ph.D. diss., Department of Hebrew and Semitic Studies, University of Wisconsin–Madison, 2002.

_____. "The Hebrew Verb: A Grammaticalization Approach." In preparation.

Dik, Simon C. *The Theory of Functional Grammar, Part 1: The Structure of the Clause.* 2d, revised ed. Edited by Kees Hengeveld. Functional Grammar Series 20. Berlin: Mouton de Gruyter, 1997.

Halliday, M. A. K. *An Introduction to Functional Grammar.* 2d ed. London: Arnold, 1994.

Joüon, Paul. *A Grammar of Biblical Hebrew.* Translated and revised by T. Muraoka. 2 vols. *Subsidia biblica* 14/1–2. Rome: Pontificio Istituto Biblico, 1993.

Long, Gary A. *Biblical Hebrew Foundations: A Concise Historical Grammar of the Phoneme through Word.* In preparation.

_____. "מחק." Pages 921–22 in vol. 2 of *New International Dictionary of Old Testament Theology and Exegesis.* Edited by W. VanGemeren. 5 vols. Grand Rapids, Mich.: Zondervan, 1997.

_____. *Old Testament Exegesis: Graduate Study Guide.* Springfield, Mo.: Global University, forthcoming.

_____. "The Written Story: Toward Understanding Text as Representation and Function." *Vetus Testamentum* 49 (1999): 165–85.

Lyons, John. *Introduction to Theoretical Linguistics.* Cambridge: Cambridge University Press, 1968.

Miller, Cynthia L. *The Representation of Speech in Biblical Hebrew Narrative: A Linguistic Analysis.* Harvard Semitic Museum Monographs 55. Atlanta: Scholars Press, 1996.

Rozelaar, M. "An Unrecognized Part of the Human Anatomy," *Judaism* 37 (1988): 97–101.

van der Merwe, Christo H. J., Jackie A. Naudé, and Jan H. Kroeze. *A Biblical Hebrew Reference Grammar.* Biblical Languages: Hebrew 3. Sheffield: Sheffield Academic Press, 1999.

Waltke, Bruce K. and M. O'Connor. *An Introduction to Biblical Hebrew Syntax.* Winona Lake, Ind.: Eisenbrauns, 1999.

INDEX OF TOPICS

D

E

J

L

M

N

183

O

P

X